CW00554049

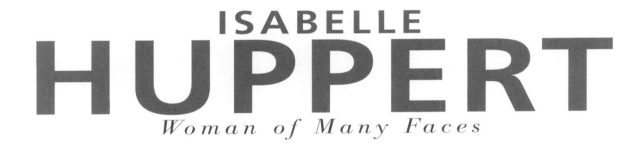

ISABELLE HUPPERT

Woman of Many Faces

TRANSLATED FROM THE FRENCH BY SIMON JONES

TRANSLATED FROM THE GERMAN BY STEVEN LINDBERG

HARRY N. ABRAMS, INC., PUBLISHERS

The photographs reproduced in this book will be exhibited in:

New York, October 2005
Paris, January 2006
Berlin, February 2006
London, May 2006
Tokyo, June 2006
Rome, September 2006
Madrid, October 2006
São Paulo, December 2006–January 2007
Beijing, June 2007

Project Manager, English-language edition: Céline Moulard
Editor, English-language edition: Nancy Cohen
Jacket design, English-language edition: Shawn Dahl
Design Coordinator, English-language edition: Shawn Dahl
Production Coordinator, English-language edition: Steve Baker
Picture research: Karine Benzaquin Laidain

Library of Congress Control Number: 2005929960

Published in 2005 by Harry N. Abrams, Incorporated, New York

Printed and bound in Italy
10 9 8 7 6 5 4 3 2 1

Harry N. Abrams, Inc.
100 Fifth Avenue
New York, N.Y. 10011
www.abramsbooks.com

Abrams is a subsidiary of
LA MARTINIÈRE

Concept by Ronald Chammah
Edited by Ronald Chammah
and Jeanne Fouchet

Antoine d'Agata, Richard Avedon, Arnaud Baumann, Carole Bellaïche, Édouard Boubat, Jean-Christian Bourcart, Guy Bourdin, Jérôme Brézillon, Henri Cartier-Bresson, Ronald Chammah, Jean-Philippe Charbonnier, Pénélope Chauvelot, Michel Comte, Roger Corbeau, Bruce Davidson, Marie-Laure de Decker, Patrick Demarchelier, Raymond Depardon, Philip-Lorca DiCorcia, Robert Doisneau, Claudine Doury, Richard Dumas, William Eggleston, Elliott Erwitt, Patrick Faigenbaum, Martine Franck, Robert Frank, Leonard Freed, Claude Gassian, Ralph Gibson, Nan Goldin, Lucien Hervé, Noelle Hoeppe, Robin Holland, Roni Horn, Frank Horvat, Dominique Issermann, Douglas Kirkland, Thomas Klausmann, Nick Knight, Josef Koudelka, Brigitte Lacombe, Jacques Henri Lartigue, William Laxton, Ange Leccia, Annie Leibovitz, Peter Lindbergh, Anne-Marie Miéville, Sarah Moon, Pete Moss, Helmut Newton, Gueorgui Pinkhassov, Sylvia Plachy, Bernard Plossu, Len Prince, Guy Le Querrec, Bettina Rheims, Marc Riboud, Herb Ritts, Karin Rocholl, Willy Ronis, Paolo Roversi, Lise Sarfati, Ferdinando Scianna, Jeanloup Sieff, Hedi Slimane, Studio Harcourt, Hiroshi Sugimoto, Juergen Teller, Michel Vanden Eeckhoudt, Pascal Victor, George Whitear, Joel-Peter Witkin, Hugues de Wurstemberger

Elfriede Jelinek, Patrice Chéreau, Susan Sontag

Foreword by
Serge Toubiana

ANONYMOUS, *1968*

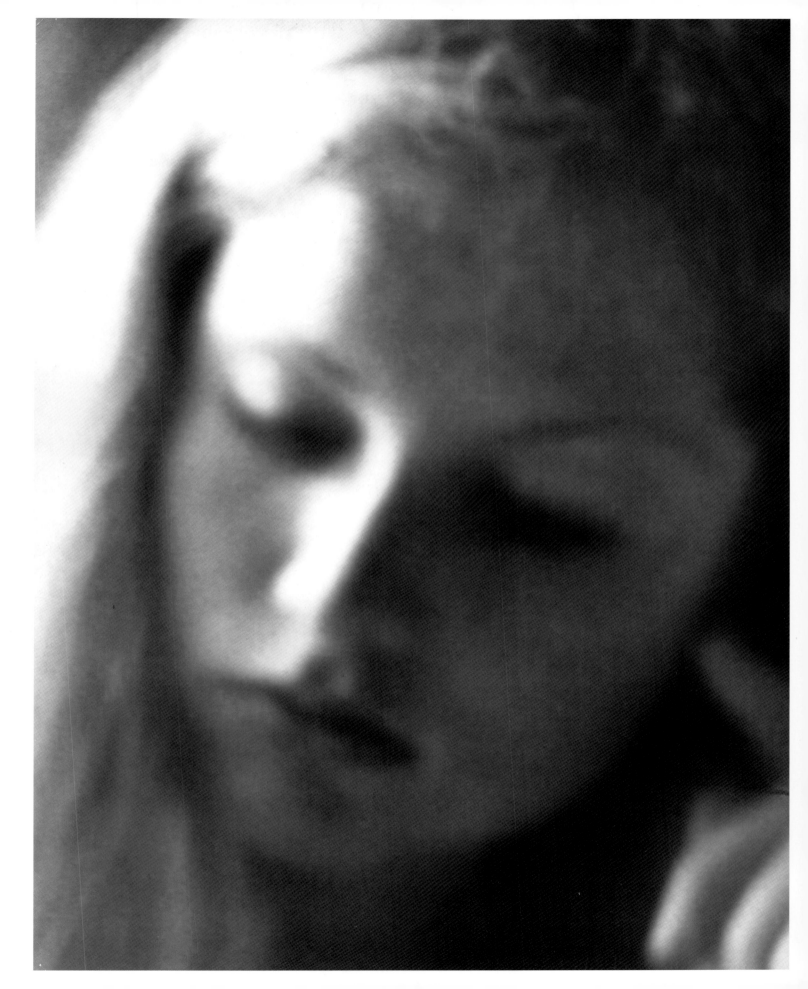

Woman of Many Faces

What I want, in short, is that my (mobile) image,
buffeted among a thousand shifting photographs, altering with
situation and age, should always coincide with my (profound)
"self"; but it is the contrary that must be said: "myself" never
coincides with my image; for it is the image which is heavy,
motionless, stubborn (which is why society sustains it), and "myself"
which is light, divided, dispersed; like a bottle-imp, "myself"
doesn't hold still, giggling in my jar: if only Photography could
give me a neutral, anatomic body, a body which signifies nothing!

ROLAND BARTHES, *Camera Lucida*[1]

Foreword

Isabelle Huppert is the most courageous among contemporary actresses when it comes to the choices she makes, both in the cinema and in the theater—choices that are guided by intelligence and by keen intuition. Her strong character always inclines her toward the riskiest course. Her boldness captivates us, as does her almost childlike determination to build herself a future as an actress. She likes to seek out the most diverse of filmmakers by making them feel it is they who have chosen her—when in fact it is often she who has chosen them. She does not play tricks or lie, but is content to let them believe what they will. Her horizons as an actress are not limited to French cinema, but encompass Europe and the rest of the world. For she fears nothing. While building an exemplary career in the name of the high ideals she applies to cinema, Isabelle Huppert has ensured that she still lives her own life. She is part of the world; she knows how to see it and grasp it, and she continually invites us to share her intimacy. Isabelle Huppert is highly skilled at inviting us to come very close to her, while at the same time keeping her distance. She does not confuse intimacy with familiarity—a distinction today's media frequently ignore or abuse. It is within this space that the acting (and also the intimate, secret self) can be born, become established, function, and do its work.

Dizziness and turmoil. In Isabelle Huppert there is a strange, singular relationship between control, or self-control, on the one hand and the unconscious and impulsive on the other. It is in this limbo, this undefined and blurred area, that she hides and reveals herself, appears and disappears. There lie the foundations of her acting—one might almost say her joy of acting. Her many and repeated appearances do not in the end lead to greater familiarity. On the contrary: They deepen the mystery, and at the same time stimulate our curiosity anew. How close are we to her? Is it not she who takes stock and decides which is the best spot before the camera lens? Photographed by so many photographers, it is she who looks at us. Adopting a passive attitude, she seems to understand photography from within. She does not fear it. That is clearly conveyed in this book, from the first glance. What fascinates us is her energy as an actress and, at the same time, her inner strength. She is generous in offering herself to be photographed, while at the same time remaining secret, almost absent, distant, as if she did not want to give all of herself, or only little by little, while taking her time. Hence the idea of infinite repetition. The multiplicity of images and poses over the course of time never exhausts the subject—quite the contrary. Through this photographic experience, unceasingly renewed, pleasure and acting remain intact. And the mystery remains whole. The same thing appears each time, but always different, reenacted, displaced, disguised. It is, so to speak, Isabelle Huppert as portrayed by herself, but through the eyes of others. Her intimate self needs to pass through this "objective" phase—the act of being photographed, in which the subject becomes an object—to exist and be visible. Roland Barthes writes that at this precise moment the "subject who feels he is becoming an object ... experience[s] a micro-version of death (of parenthesis) ... truly becoming a specter."[2]

The enigma of Isabelle Huppert is placed there, before the lens, just to the saturation point. The photographers come and go, but she remains. This behavior on the part of authors (photographers in this case) in the end reinforces the secret tactic of the subject being photographed, who is, in a sense, their model. We are witnessing a reversal of the relationship between the subject who is being viewed and the subject who is doing the viewing, to borrow the terminology Barthes uses in *Camera Lucida*. Her apparent passivity is her way of taking action.

It is like a game or an obsession, a childlike pleasure that becomes a fixation: to be photographed by as many photographers as possible, to become the object of an imaginary, dispersed collection that this book, as a singular object, gathers together. Over the years Isabelle Huppert has come across virtually every photographer on the planet, from the "veterans" to the great "humanists," such as Henri Cartier-Bresson, Édouard Boubat,

Robert Doisneau, Roger Corbeau, Jacques Henri Lartigue, Richard Avedon, Guy Bourdin, Willy Ronis, Marc Riboud, Josef Koudelka, and Helmut Newton, to the artists of modern photography, among them Antoine d'Agata, Ange Leccia, and Philip-Lorca Di Corcia. The list is long and still unfinished.

This photographic experience therefore covers a very broad spectrum, both in historical or generational terms—for, from Lartigue to Leccia, almost a century of photography passes before our eyes—and in terms of form and style. This vast iconic sample also covers various genres: fashion photography, film photography—both classic (the Harcourt style) and "star system" style-reportage, and photography with a "plastic" bent, inspired by video and digital installations.

Beyond the different styles and genres, beyond the signatures of individual photographers, each of these photographs invites us to ask the same question: What secret lies behind this semblance of the neutral? For Isabelle Huppert, pleasure or delight appears at the moment when the light that is born of her acting, her face, and her voice imperceptibly illuminates the areas of shadow that attract it and which it wants to pierce—like a child who is not afraid of the dark. Her destiny is mapped out: To act as often as possible, as long as possible, is a way of resisting the march of time, by inventing for herself another life, many parallel lives. This book of images invites us to join in that game of hide-and-seek.

Her energy and strength are sometimes concealed behind a sort of melancholy, opacity, or neutrality—an absence, or a dream of being elsewhere. It is this crack that the greatest photographers have been able to capture, with her complicity. When she seems to let herself go in front of the lens, it is in fact she who is taking control, she who is watching us. One day Cartier-Bresson went to photograph her at her home. And there, on her couch, she absented or abandoned herself. Often her eyes were closed. Sometimes she slept. It is her way of working. What is she thinking about? What inner journey is she making at the exact moment the shutter is released? It is impossible to know. It is her method, her intimate strategy—which always works—to thwart the photographic demand. I am willing to be photographed on the condition that I can be absent. Please act as if I were here—I know that I am not, really. What you are going to photograph is me when I am not here.

We can see that she and the photographers share a common language, a tacit understanding, a form of mutual, implicit respect founded on the love of the image and of the photographic journey. Each thinks he or she grasps an intimate part of the other. It is a pact between the public image and the secret soul that this fine book on

Isabelle Huppert reveals to us. To be present in order not to be: That is what this actress seems to be telling us, by constantly playing with appearance and its mechanical repetition. Sometimes she looks straight at the lens, as if to settle once and for all our spectator's turmoil (as, for example, in the work of Jean-Philippe Charbonnier, Édouard Boubat, Patrick Demarchelier, and others). This is the case in photographs in which she bares part of her body (see the portraits by Jeanloup Sieff and Helmut Newton). Her cameralike gaze seems like a challenge, erasing any ideas of voyeurism: You want to see my body, but it is my soul that I reveal. The art of displacement: You will know nothing of me, because it is I who am looking at you. Sometimes she looks beyond the frame, thus broadening her horizon. Then she invites us to imagine an unknown space, which she alone knows, and tells us in passing to look elsewhere. In this double game Isabelle Huppert, although passive and dreamy, always emerges the winner.

SERGE TOUBIANA

Notes

1. *Camera Lucida: Reflections on Photography*, trans. Richard Howard. New York: Hill and Wang, 1981, p. 12. Originally published as *La Chambre claire: Note sur la photographie*. Paris: Cahiers du cinéma/Gallimard/Seuil, 1980.

2. *Camera Lucida*, p. 14.

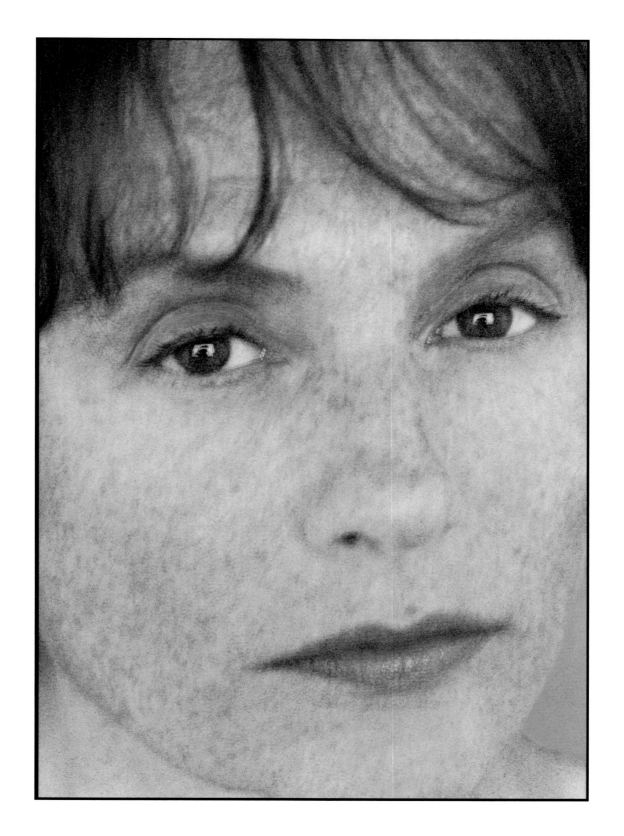

SARAH MOON, *2001*

15

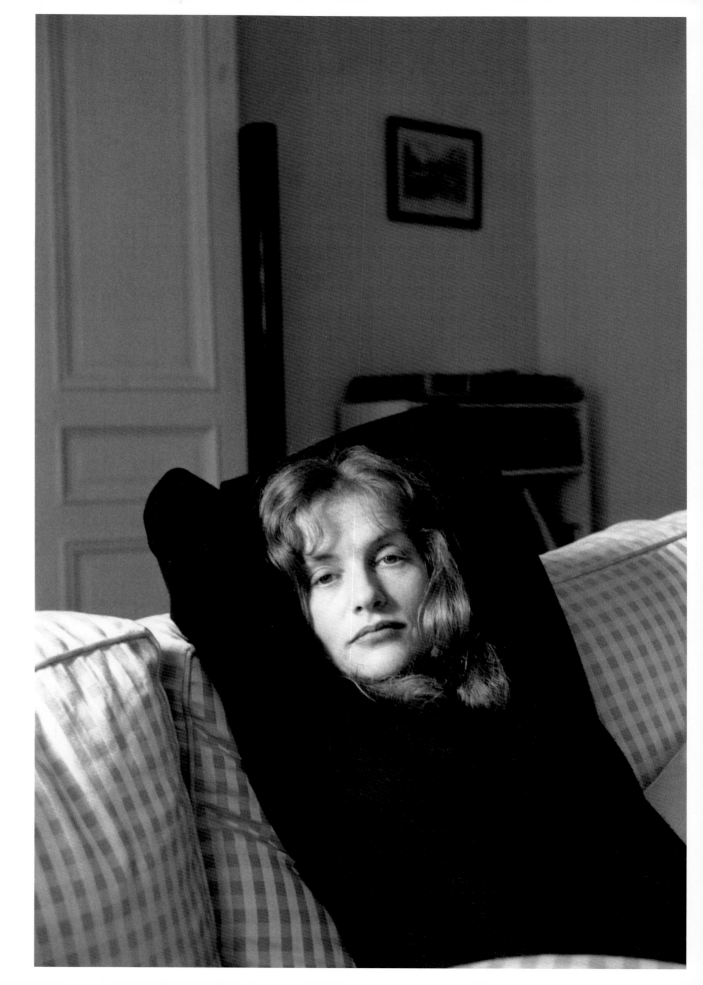

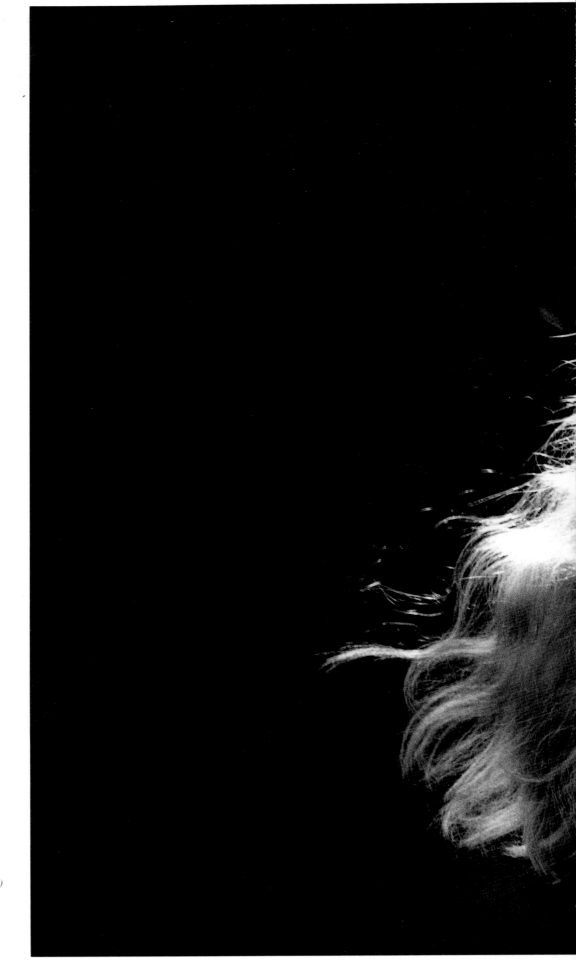

KARIN ROCHOLL, *1990*

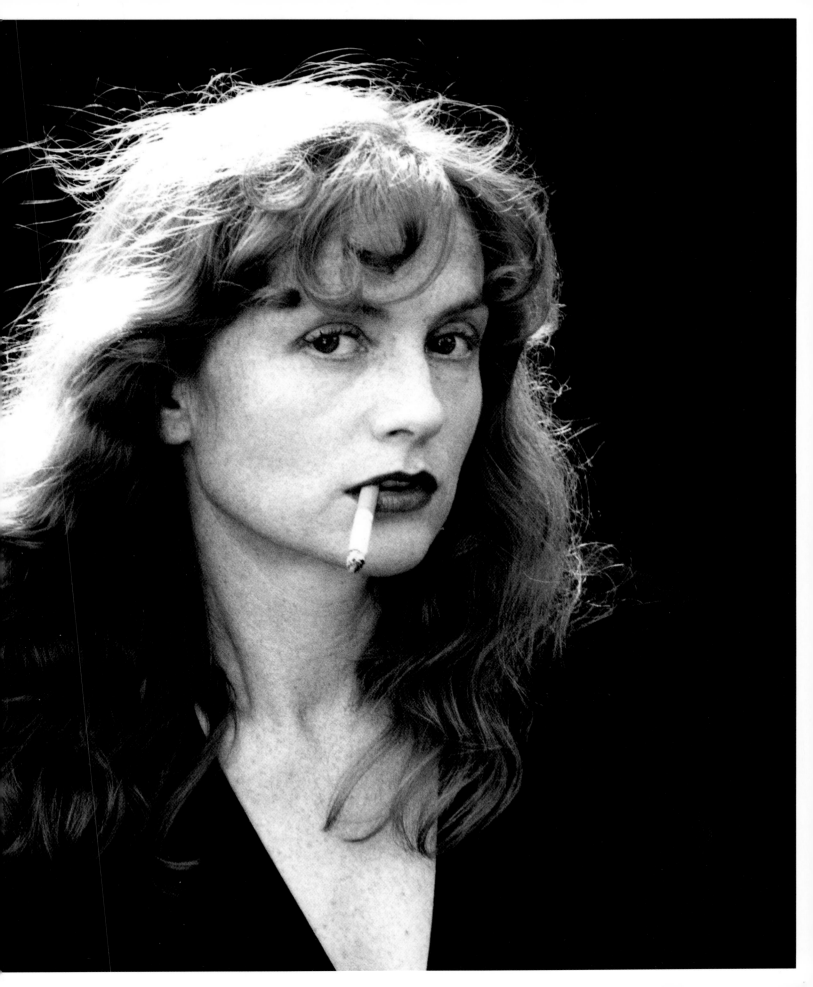

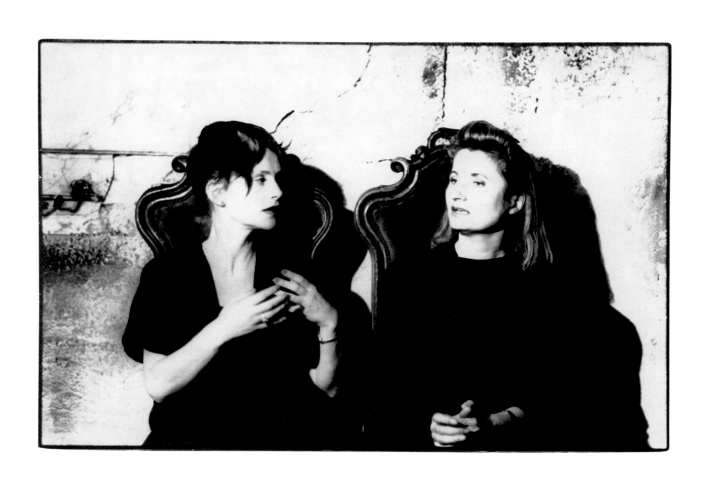

THOMAS KLAUSMANN, *1990*

The Defenseless Face

ELFRIEDE JELINEK

When it looks at you, Isabelle Huppert's face destroys its own contradiction, which it had incarnated until that moment. Positive and negative in one. This film no longer needs to be developed. This actress is one who is always completely present and at the same time not there at all. It makes no sense that she clings to her face because she doesn't have to run anywhere. She knows from the outset that she cannot maintain her face, because as soon as it portrays something it dissolves again, and at the same time it dissolves the contradiction, even its self-contradiction. Perhaps that's what acting is: showing how one constantly contradicts oneself even when one concedes. Resisting oneself. This actress's face defends itself against an imaginary opponent precisely because it turns out to be defenseless. What happens is not that one woman becomes another whom she is supposed to portray; rather, her face, in which all this is meant to be reflected, surrenders itself, without any trace of effort. That doesn't mean her face refuses to accept or even tolerate a contradiction; it simply doesn't see one. Even makeup contradicts this face, which is, time and again, perfectly un-made-up, yet—confronted with the persistent rubbing by stylists and makeup artists—does not defend itself. It is defenseless because it is the face of an actress whose work exists not in struggle, not in resistance. This face confesses everything. And this face wants to do everything itself. It wants to make amends. It protests any inconsistency: for example, in painting on another face (as the role requires) while at the same time asserting itself, so it can become another face (in which case it doesn't have to assert itself; it's simply there, isn't it?), so it can slip into the role, as they say.

Both this face's self-assertion and its assertion lie on its absolute defenselessness. Without being submissive, it yields itself, but it doesn't just yield: It yields to everything that is demanded of it. In this case, the parasitic role breaks its way out from within—at least I believe so; I can only believe, as it remains a mystery—to forge features and mimicry; it isn't plastered from the outside onto the face to be seen there but rather comes from inside. This actress's face is just as defenseless from inside as it is from outside; it is made to be penetrated. But from the outside it intensely resists being reworked. Resistance in powerlessness: another contradiction? Only seemingly. This face is never made up; even when it's made up, it's not made up, so that it can work out from inside, so that something can "work its way out" from inside, so that a personality other than that of the actress can be worked out, can be worked out by itself, as if of its own accord. If any handling charges fall due thereby, can they be levied (and then collected)? Actors often say that they have "profited" from a role, that is, learned something for their own lives from having studied a character. Does this actress now simply go home with her day's earnings, unchanged, unchangeable? Unmoved, and us forever excluded? Our voyeuristic gazes at the stage or screen are serenely returned, not even cast back in anger. We have laid claim to the face of this film star, but it has not been granted to us. This face should be illuminated from inside just for us. It has soaked up the spotlights, and now they pour out again as light and shadow. Light, yes, but in the sense of clearing up (a process that cannot be controlled by will), and not a shedding of light. Perhaps this face tolerates no reworking, including explanatory ones (our interpretation?), because that would interfere with this clarity, which does not enhance any interpretation, luminous as it is. Rather, it's simply like this: This face is a face that could belong to anyone and only happens to belong to Isabelle Huppert. She has picked it up. She has picked it for herself but not for us. This process of clearing up, which is not (or perhaps is only seemingly) based on an effort of will, thus becomes the elucidation, the ceaseless illumination of new existences, depending on the role. But this light is firmly mounted under her skin, so that the portrayal can get under others' skin. Her face cannot be painted, even though it often is; I assert that it is always un-made-up, because part of its truth is that one can recognize oneself simultaneously with the truth of the character being portrayed, and can also perceive this actress's own existence as opening the way for the truth, for any truth. Huppert does not establish a connection to anything. Any connection we may have to her is one that we ourselves—someone other than her—have constructed, and she has serenely taken it up. She has taken it lying down.

It simply isn't so that in the end the truth always gains acceptance, as some claim. Poor truth: It always has to bring itself to light, and to bring something else, something beyond itself, something like a perception. The truth will out. Or won't it? But what will it drag along with it? In the case of this actress, it seems to me, the truth is brought out from inside; it comes to her through her face, without having to do anything to it. Her face is the bridge that the truth must cross; it has no other choice. The truth must out, and nothing can stop it, because it drills out from within, so to speak, in order to draw itself out. And this drawing is not what children do, copying or tracing something that already exists. This drawing out is a substantial and yet insubstantial process of existence itself, one that is cleared up when it says the truth. The truth about another person who isn't who she is. A character who is supposed to be portrayed. Isabelle Huppert is always an actress in photographs—even in those in which she poses, highly stylized, beautifully dressed, as a model for fashion photographers—and as an actress she is perhaps a kind of signature key to which all the other keys relate and to which they all eventually must return for something to come to a close, as in the classical theory of harmony. Tonic, dominant (without dominating; it is dominated by the tonic toward which everything strains; the strain is unnecessary; it has to be brought back to the initial key to come to a close, and this closure is always an opening at the same time), perhaps the subdominant as well, a few more choice tortures, and then again: back to the beginning, come to a rest. And then back again and repeat, so that this face, and with it the character, can finally come to a close—and correctly so. True closure means no one has to do anything more to it. It's simply closed. No sign is necessary. Isabelle Huppert is—since *The Lacemaker*—a closed actress who gives everything but takes nothing in order to give. The closing of a defenseless, un-made-up face can result from a number of different closure mechanisms (which can always be added afterward, if one is frightened by something else—perhaps by a real transformation—so that the face is painted, but always afterward), but it always falls back into the tonic, the initial key. With Isabelle Huppert, however, this initial key is always seen as being of a type that befits her (no type is possible for her other than that of variation, but on the condition of returning to the beginning, no matter how long Ariadne's thread and how large the labyrinth). The possibility of transforming into a character other than herself is always an internal possibility for Isabelle Huppert, never an external one. The actress as true subject, even as she transforms into other subjects. And the more she is placed into relation with her fellow actors, by a script that was realized by a team, the more she asserts her character as a subject. In this case, however, the assertion is unnecessary. Something is being knocked on, but it isn't a door. This woman needs neither self-assertiveness nor presence of mind; she comes neither before the fall nor after the fall. She is simply there, but she cannot be used, not even for the role. That is why being un-made-up is precisely her true state of rest—not, however, the initial state, as it is with many other actresses, an initial state that is immediately followed by something. Other actresses are almost impossible to imagine un-made-up. Isabelle Huppert can only be imagined un-made-up, with a purpose: so that she can become that other person. Even a simple hat or cap would be too much. Not having anything on is her true state of composure, so that something can come out. Because this actress, who really is an actress (and not just a beautiful woman who portrays one thing or another, preferably the One, the Only, the Role per se), can thus be everything, if not perhaps everything and everyone—precisely not that, as otherwise makeup would be essential for her. Because this actress is herself (and thus at the same time everything else), she exists in her roles right up close to the woman she is supposed to be portraying. She is the difference. She stands for something that isn't she who is it. She doesn't just portray it; she is it. Because we see this difference so clearly in her, she is able to retain her true existence even as she lets go of it, allowing herself to be determined by the many possibilities of existence that are demanded of an actress so that she will offer us these possibilities. She looks like she could never be determined by anything, but she is very determined, and with the determination of a somnambulist she knows what she must do; by seeming to do nothing at all, she can at any time be undetermined and consequently declare herself one who will never be determined by anyone or anything. The actress as the ultimate subject. Yes. Perhaps one could say: As long as this actress is always herself, indeed, as long as she is still herself, everything that she plays, that she portrays, can be determined as something that must be there, thus and not otherwise, because this actress herself—thus and not otherwise, precisely as she must be—is there. This type of being there allows a view of how subjective the subject is. It transforms. It remains the same. But it doesn't remain the same. For what? So that we will find our way back again to a genuine truth that was always more genuine than the one others found? Isabelle Huppert is already there.

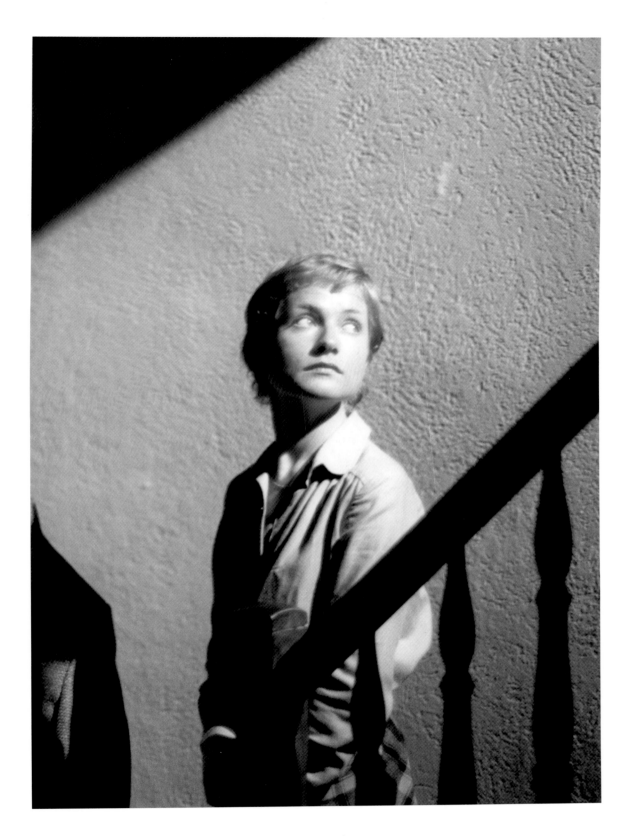

ANNE-MARIE MIÉVILLE, *1981*

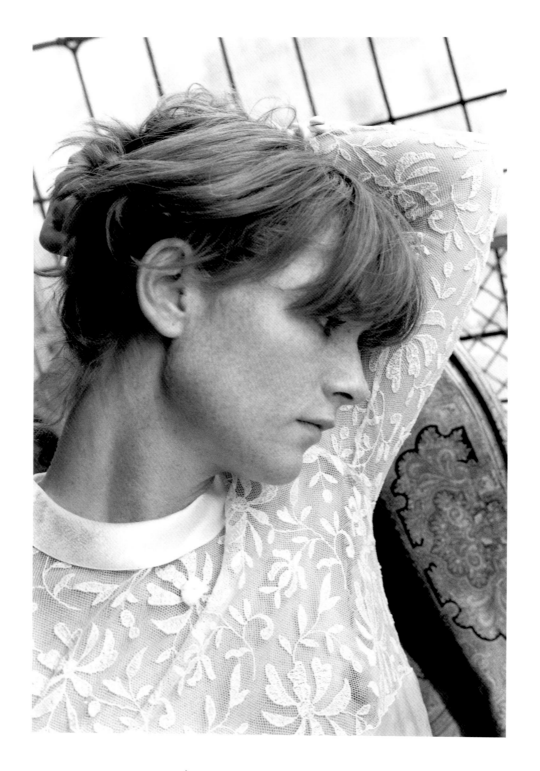

ÉDOUARD BOUBAT, *1985*

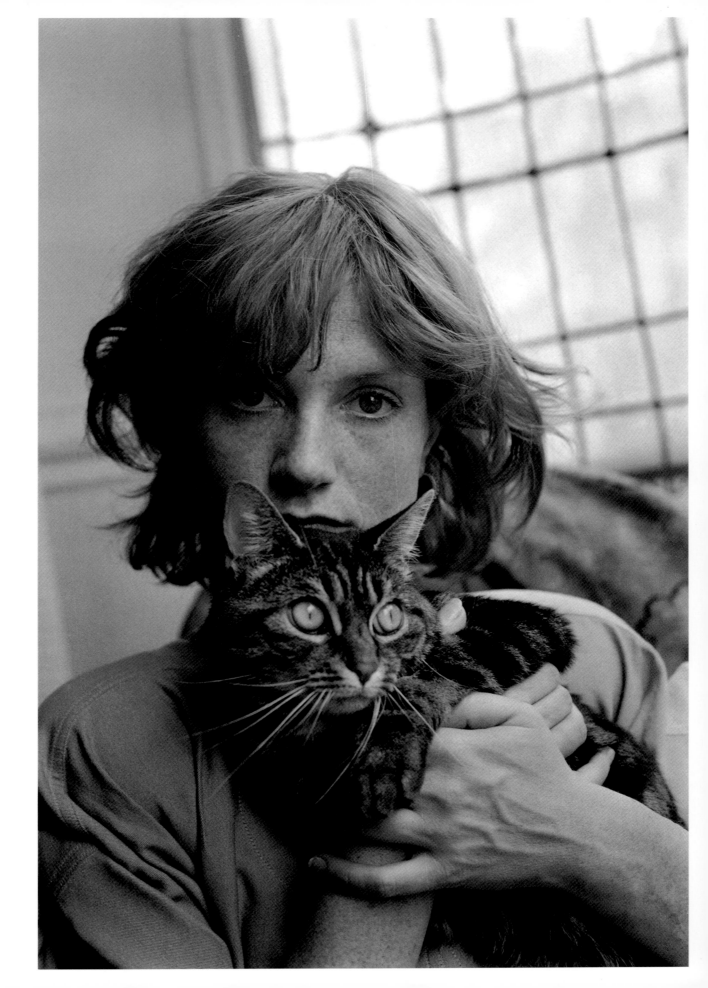

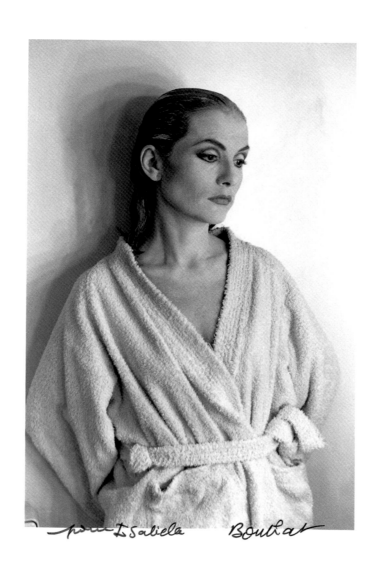

ÉDOUARD BOUBAT. *1992, 1986*

32

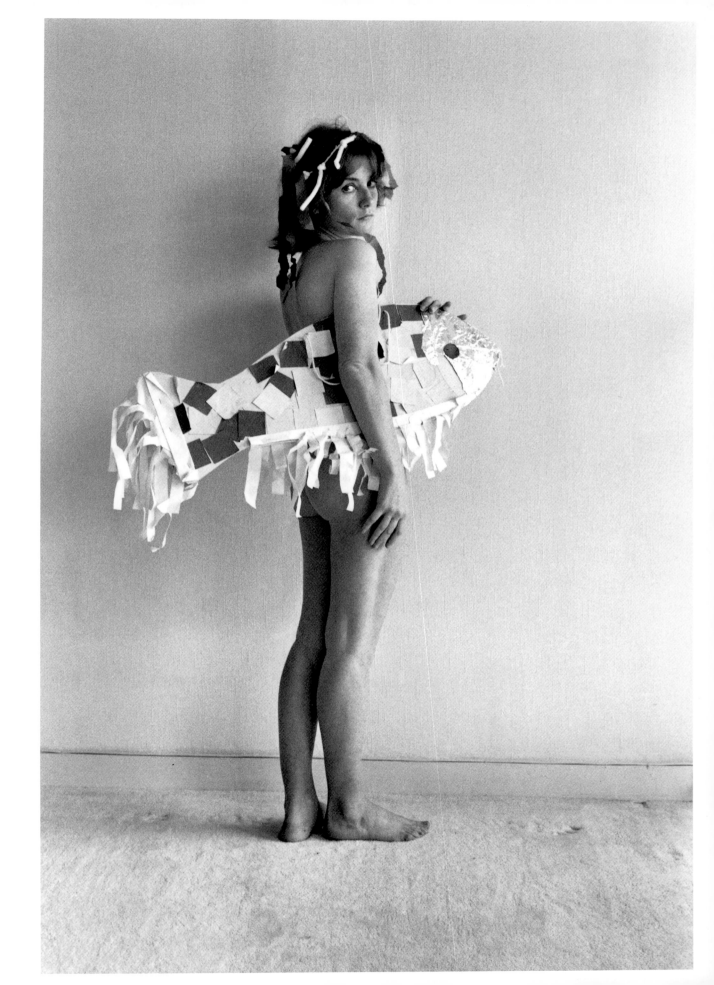

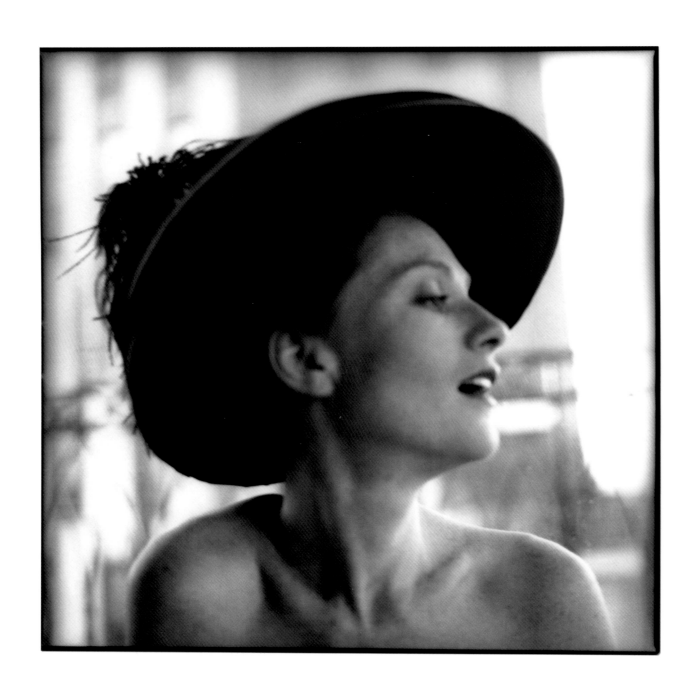

SYLVIA PLACHY, *1986*

The Abyss as Blank Page

PATRICE CHÉREAU

Salvation lies with others,
though solitude may taste like opium.[1]

ADAM ZAGAJEWSKI

The actor's job is a terrifying one. Isabelle Huppert is both intimate and distant, intelligent, cold, burning—and prepared to do anything to act. She gives herself to others while at the same time is absent; she is solitary and multiple in nature. One might say that this is true of all actresses. But in Isabelle there is something like a fatal eagerness she has taken upon herself. Is this a tragic trait? Perhaps: eagerness as destiny. She is there before us as we know her: ready to take all risks, intrepid, and with a desperation to be always present in people's minds. Again and again.

We might recall the ancient Roman actor who performed in the works of Seneca and in the great tragedies and who, it was said, carried onstage every day the urn containing his son's ashes, to summon up emotion. What ashes does Isabelle carry around with her every day? These ashes, at once burning and still, she seems to bring back to life very gently, with a calm coolness that leaves us dumbstruck. Isabelle passes through the flames looking as if she does not know what flames are. Like the phoenix, she is not consumed by them: No, she appears to emerge from them as if regenerated and transformed. Transformed: Isabelle can be everything and everywhere. She has the unsettling gift of ubiquity. Anyone who is even slightly acquainted with her knows there is something in her that devours and at the same time devours itself—a conscious, assumed narcissism that fascinates, as did the gaze of the legendary deity into whose face, it was said, one must not look.

But we should look at Isabelle carefully, and directly in the face, first of all because we do not mean to offend her, but also because sometimes we see there another Isabelle— a more fragile person whom it is possible to destabilize. It is that Isabelle, of course, who is the more delightful to my eyes, even though she appears only fleetingly in those extraordinary photographs that seem to be the result of a perfect, double process of control—by her and by the photographer, or photographers, in whose world she seems to flow, falsely docile and always herself.

How can it be that someone who is always working is afraid of not working? Perhaps it is a sort of (permanent?) dissatisfaction, something like the exhausting accomplishments—almost nonaccomplishments or empty accomplishments—of those who bleed themselves dry. This is what makes her dear to me, and close.

One day after we had made a film together, I told her that she resembled Garbo. She was not in the least surprised; indeed, to my astonishment, she agreed completely. Yes, she too is exactly this: a storm in the void. As she put it once: "to say nothing of what one is for fear of losing oneself; to hide among images of oneself." Isabelle is an abyss around which she allows us to write: Isabelle Huppert, the abyss as blank page.

Of course, we cannot completely know—or, dare I say, fully survey—an actress from just one film. We can just divine the contours, the fault lines, a few precipices, a general topography, some mysterious valleys. Neither can we do so from a hundred photographs, even by the greatest photographers, as here, where they are gathered together in thrilling abundance. For a film director like me, there is something dizzying about contemplating these thousand manifestations of a multiple, irreducible, and carnivorous self. Yes, we rediscover this here with her, in this book filled with unbridled and necessary narcissism. To be an actress, to act, is indeed to submit to destiny.

1. Translated by Clare Cavanagh in *Where the Stress Falls*, by Susan Sontag.

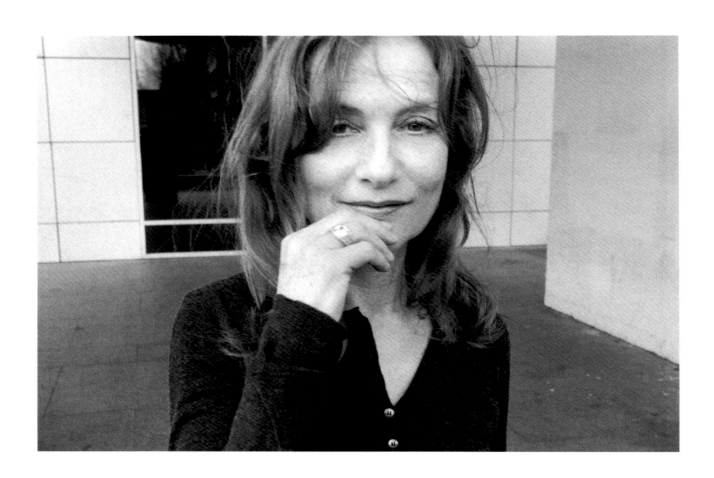

ROBERT FRANK, *2005*

38

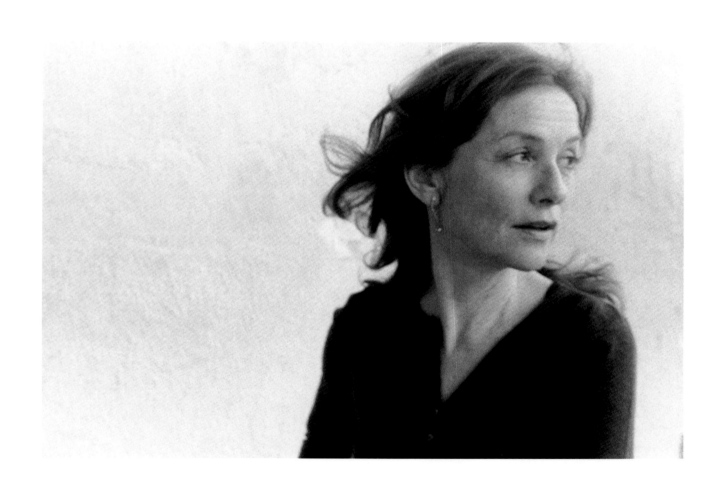

ROBERT FRANK, *2005*

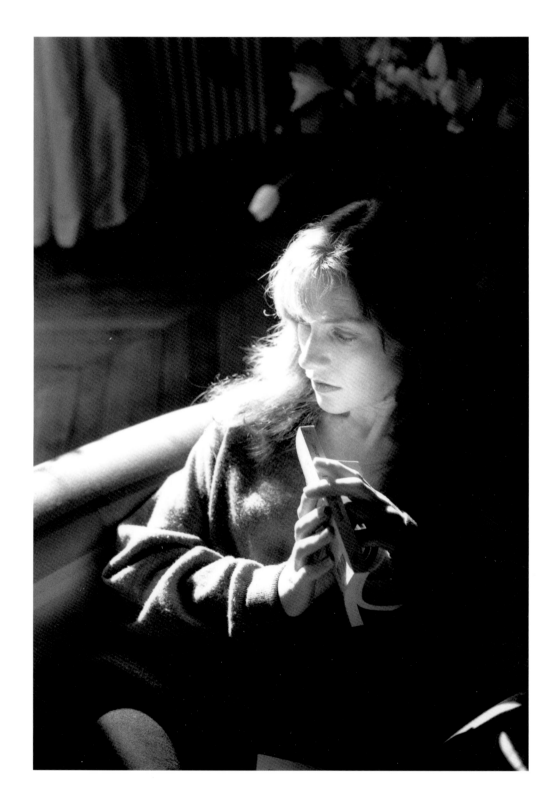

WILLY RONIS, *1994*

SUSAN SONTAG

For Isabelle.

I grew up in the American provinces, in the American Southwest. And when I was a child, thinking of growing up and of where I wanted to live, I couldn't decide whether I wanted to live in New York or Paris. Those were the two ideas of paradise for me. I luckily got to do both for large periods of my life. I do live in New York, but I certainly consider Paris my second city. I have spent a huge amount of my adult life there, and it's been my pleasure to think of France and French culture and, perhaps more actively than any other part of French culture, French cinema as central to my life....

Isabelle Huppert ... is an actor of unlimited ability, with what looks like already a very long career, a career I consider to be, at most, at midpoint—a body of work and a talent from which we can expect anything in the future, anything and everything.

I would like to mention five attributes of this great actor that make her such a formidable and exemplary presence. I mention them in no particular order, although the very fact that I must give them in a certain order perhaps betrays a certain partly indefensible personal bias. So I will list these five characteristics that I think make for a kind of total artist, a total artist in the most admirable sense.

The first quality that I would mention is beauty. That's not usually the first thing that one mentions, but I think I have an ancient Greek rather than a Christian view of beauty. I think beauty is a virtue—that's a pagan view, not a Christian view, but for me beauty is a virtue. And this is a person who exemplifies an extraordinary physical beauty, something that matters to us a lot in actors, and a lot more than sometimes we are willing to acknowledge consciously.

Then of course, number two: There's something called talent, and what is talent? Talent is, above all, expressiveness, eloquence, the capacity for expressiveness.

Third—I say this is in no particular order and yet I can't, as I say, help feeling that some sort of perverse order is involved in the fact that I list them in the way that I do. After beauty, talent or expressiveness, the third I would call intelligence. Intelligence is not a quality that one thinks is necessarily present in a creative constellation. In fact it's very often said you don't have to be intelligent to be a great artist or a great actor. I think great actors are extremely intelligent and I have never met a more intelligent actor, a more intelligent person who is an actor, than Isabelle Huppert.

Fourth: I would mention her fearlessness as an artist, as an actor. And by fearlessness I also mean something very strong. I mean something that contains a large element of ferocity, avidity, appetite, availability, risk taking—a tremendous amount of risk taking.

And last, what may seem to be the opposite pole of the first virtue I mentioned, beauty: her integrity. Her integrity as an artist and—this I can testify as someone who knows her as a friend—her integrity as a human being. So it is an honor and a pleasure to have the occasion to express my love and affection, admiration, for this great artist, for this great actor.

Adapted from a presentation at the French Institute/Alliance Française's
Trophée des Arts Gala honoring Isabelle Huppert, New York, November 5, 2003.

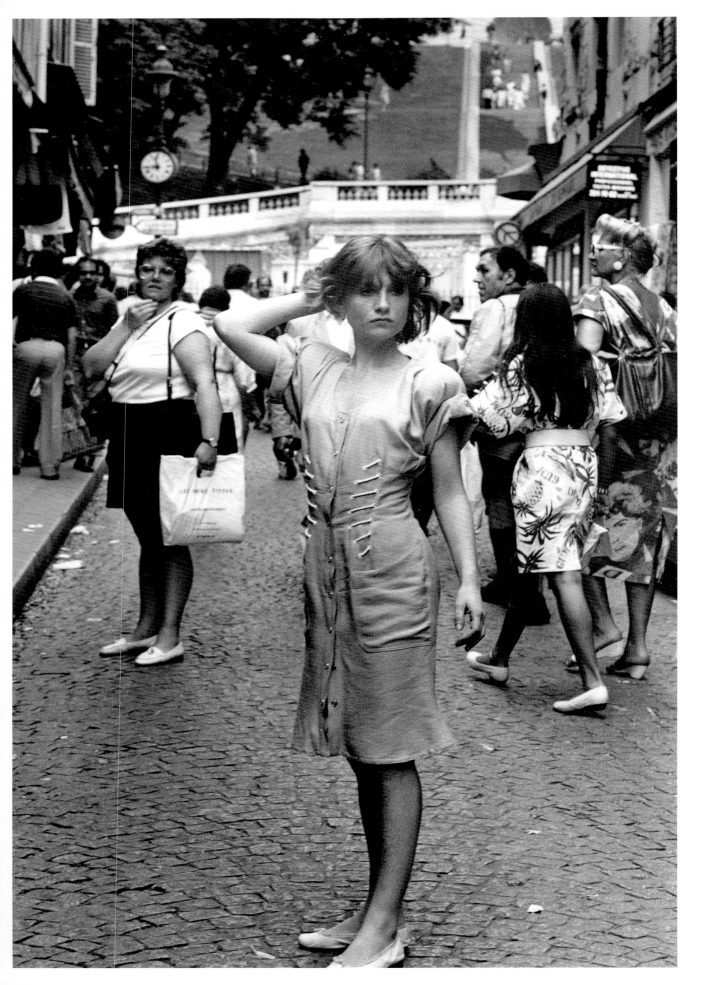

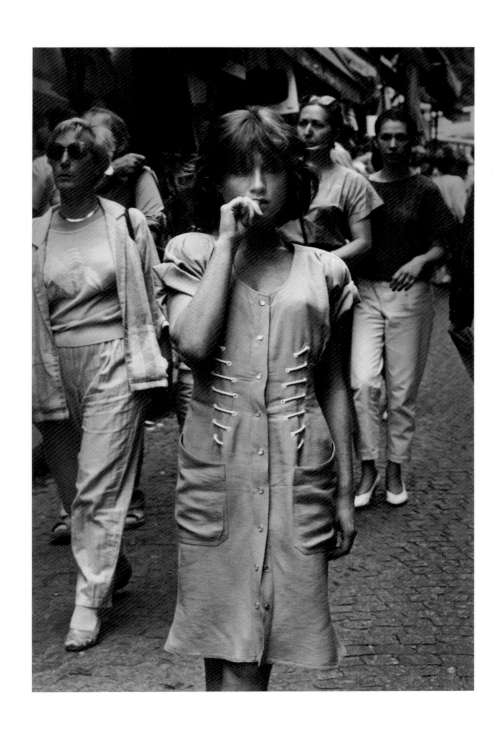

ROBERT DOISNEAU, *1985*

45

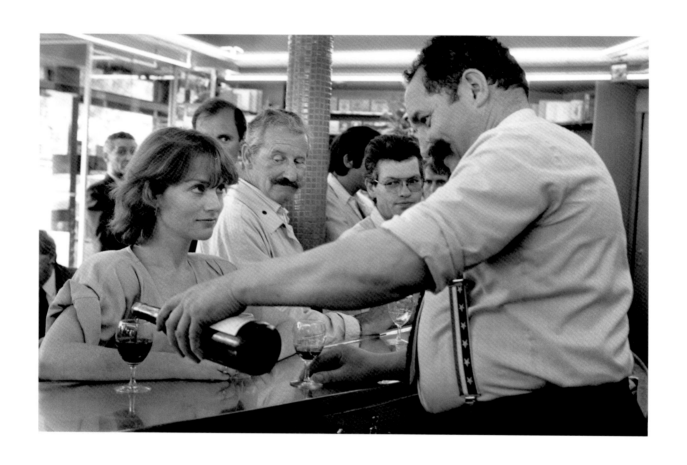

ROBERT DOISNEAU, *1985*

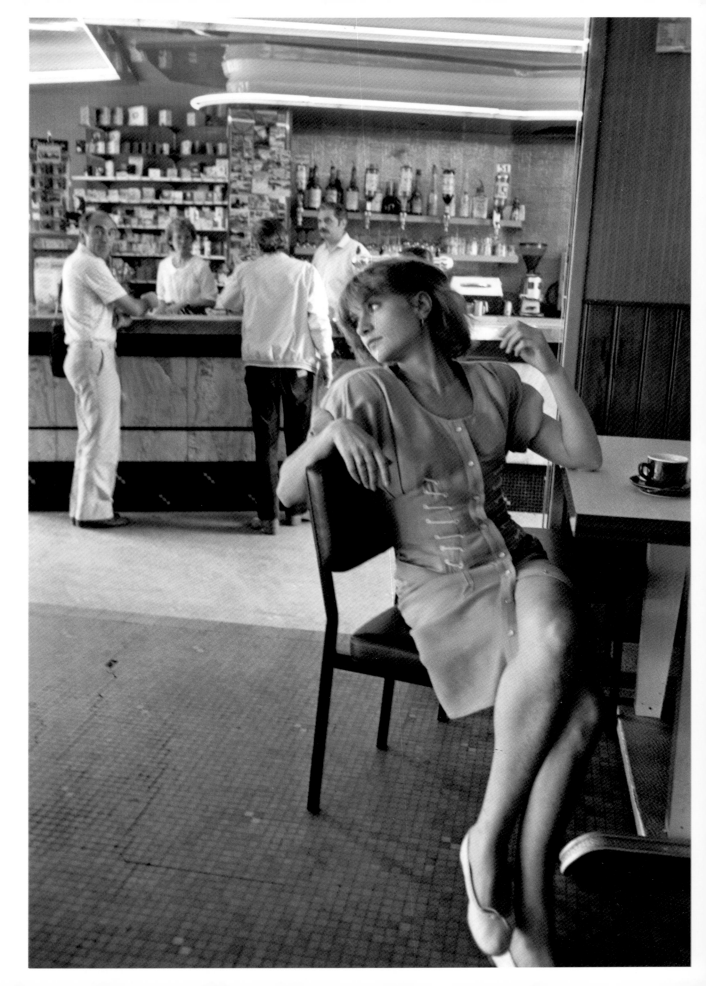

JOSEF KOUDELKA, *1985*

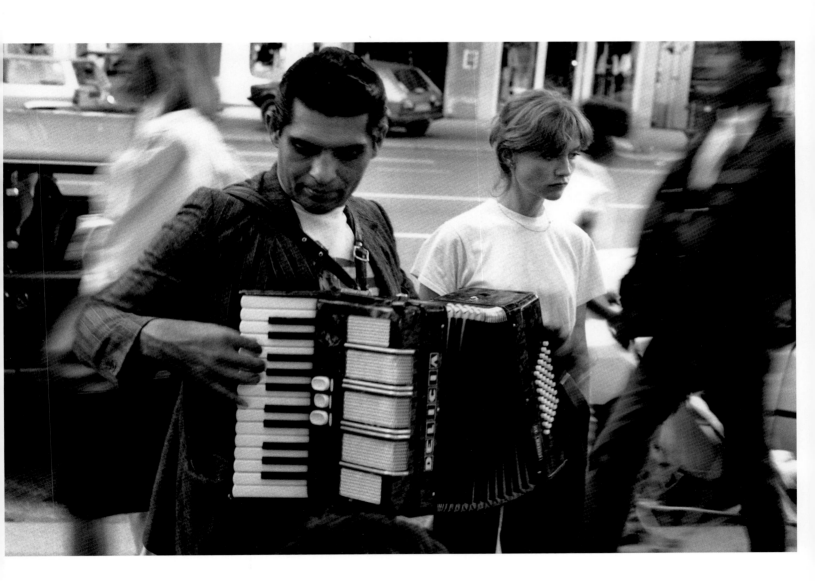

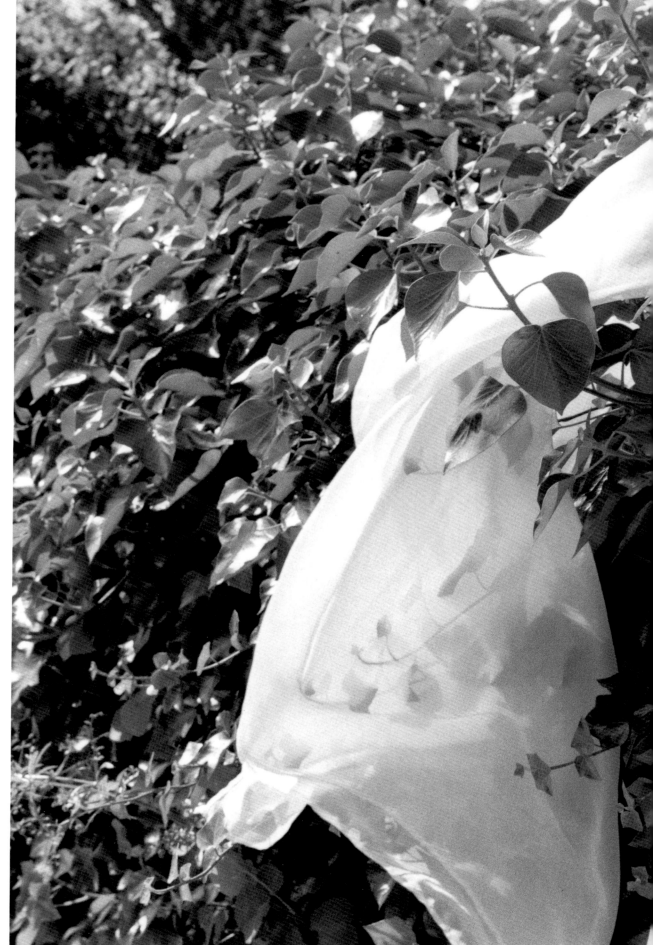

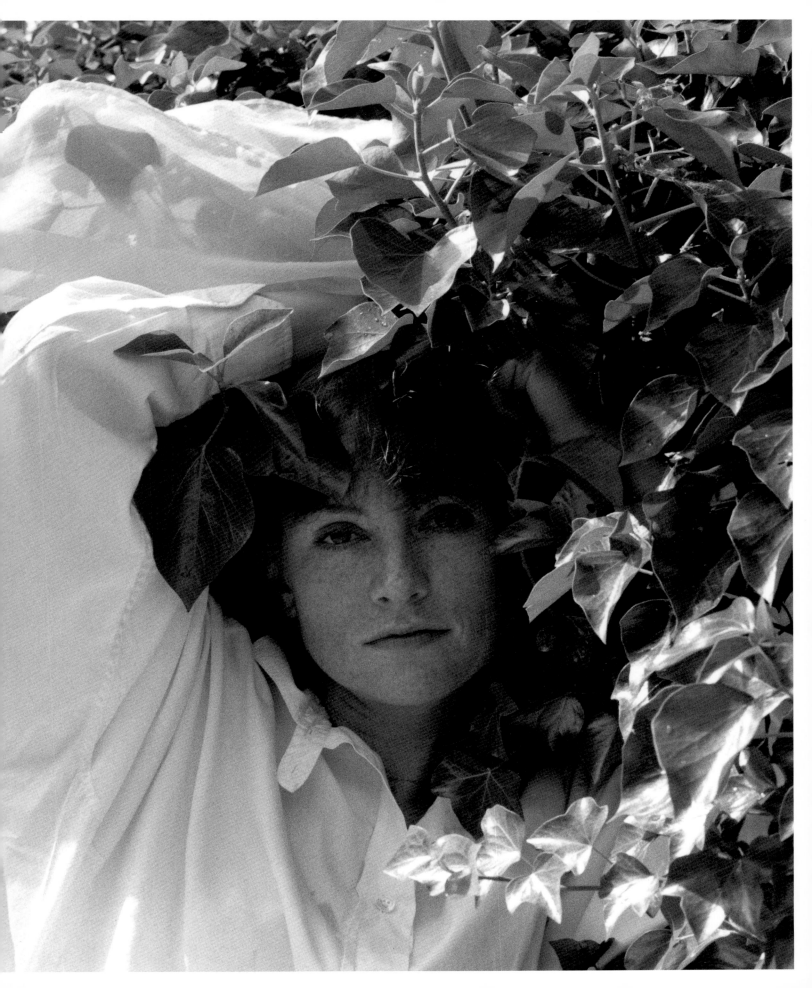

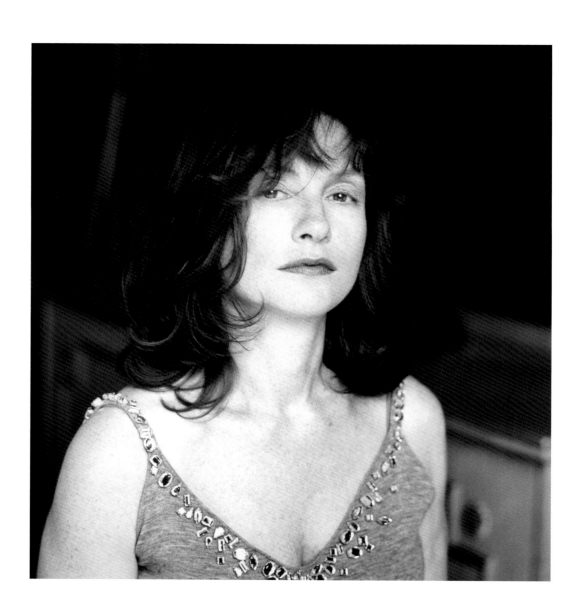

CAROLE BELLAÏCHE, *2001*

52

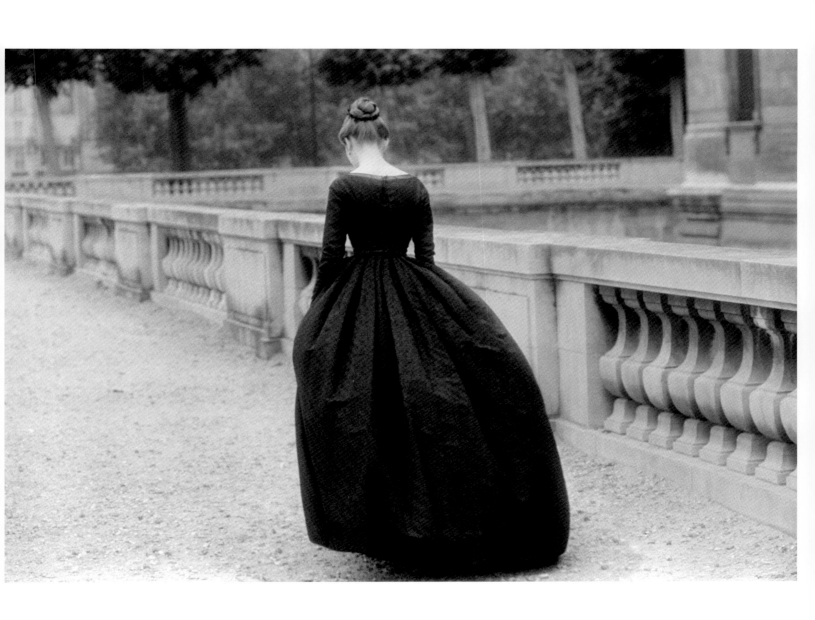

DOMINIQUE ISSERMANN, *1981*

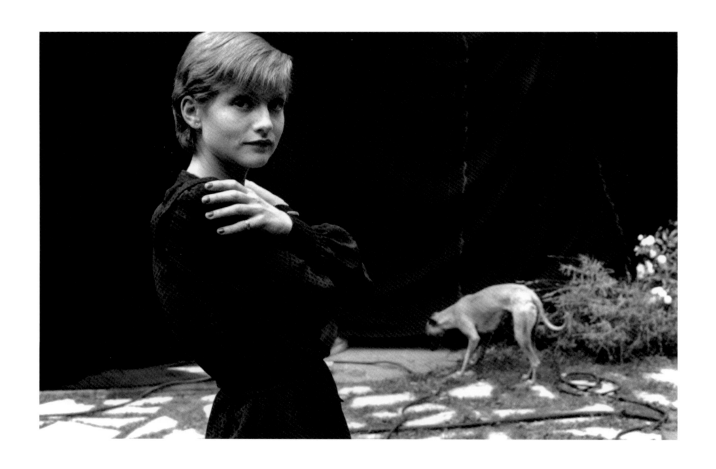

MARTINE FRANCK. *1982*

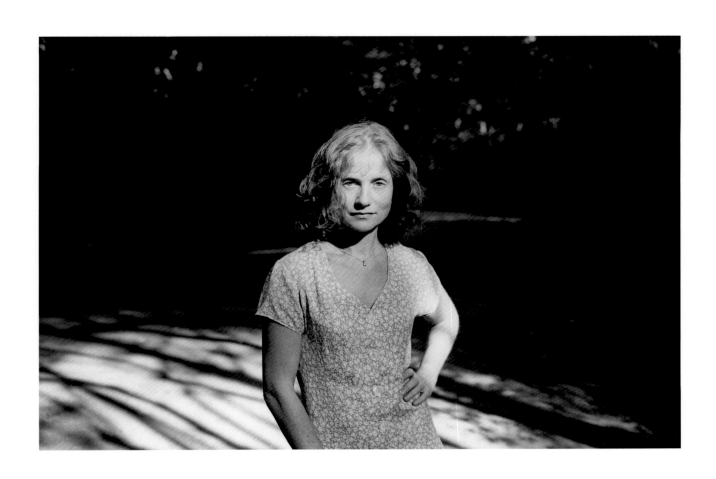

CAROLE BELLAÏCHE, *1994*

55

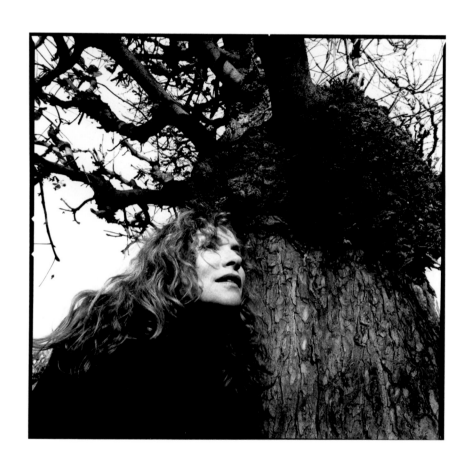

BRUCE DAVIDSON, *2004*
CLAUDE GASSIAN, *2002*

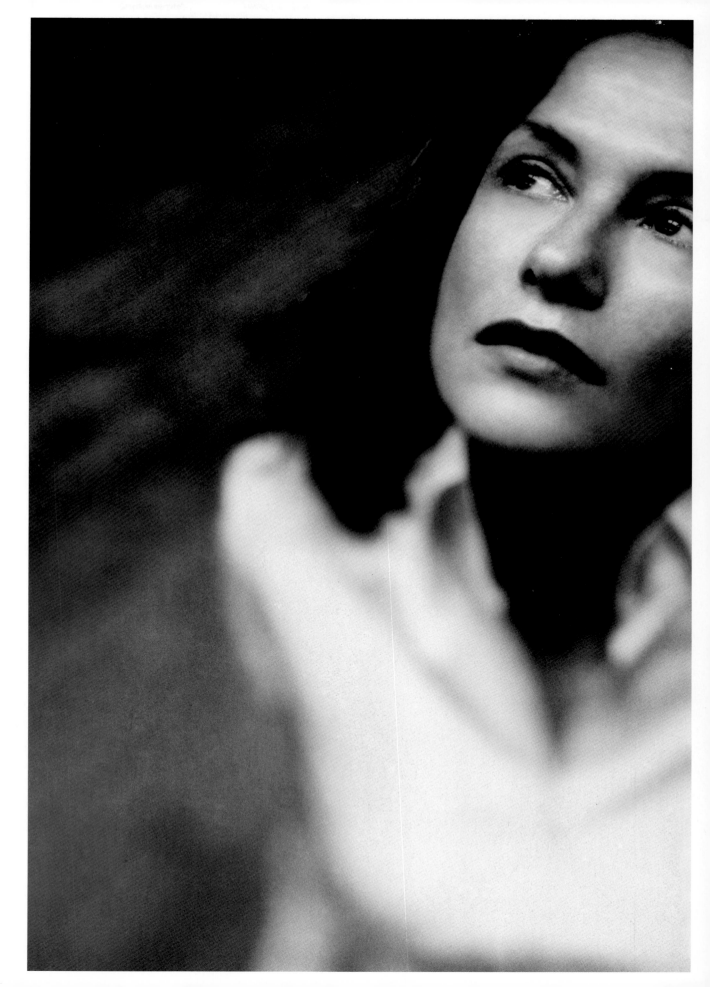

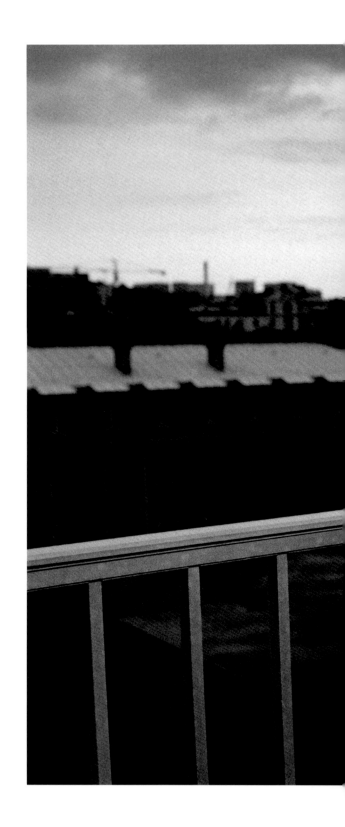

JEAN-PHILIPPE CHARBONNIER, *1984*

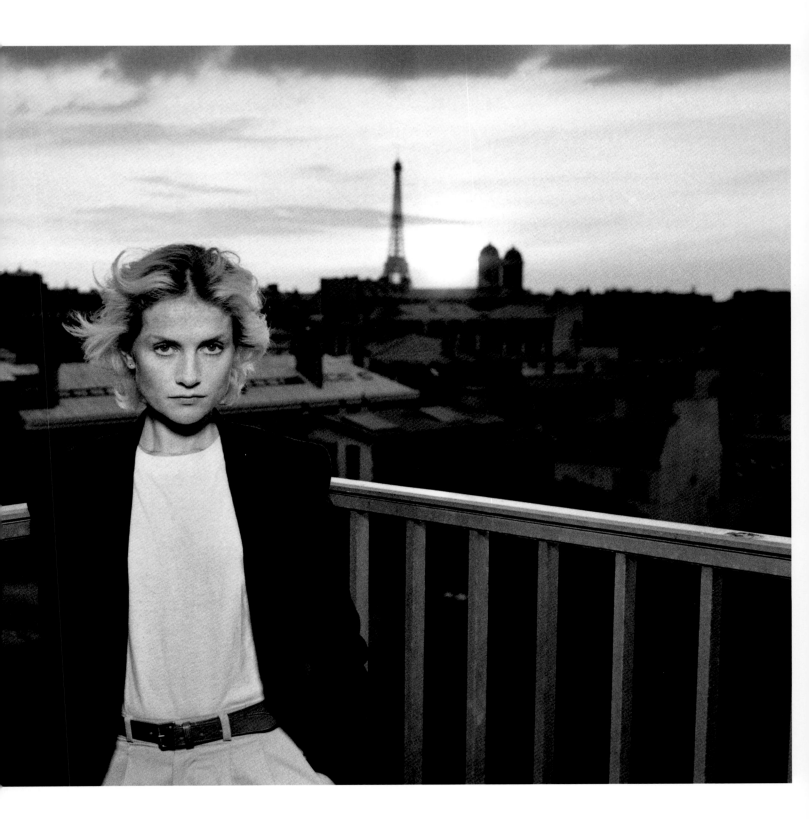

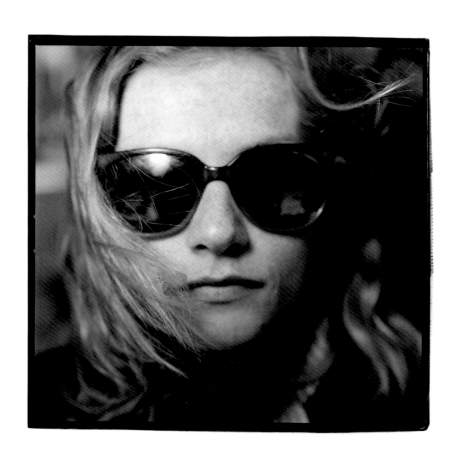

SYLVIA PLACHY, *1986*

60

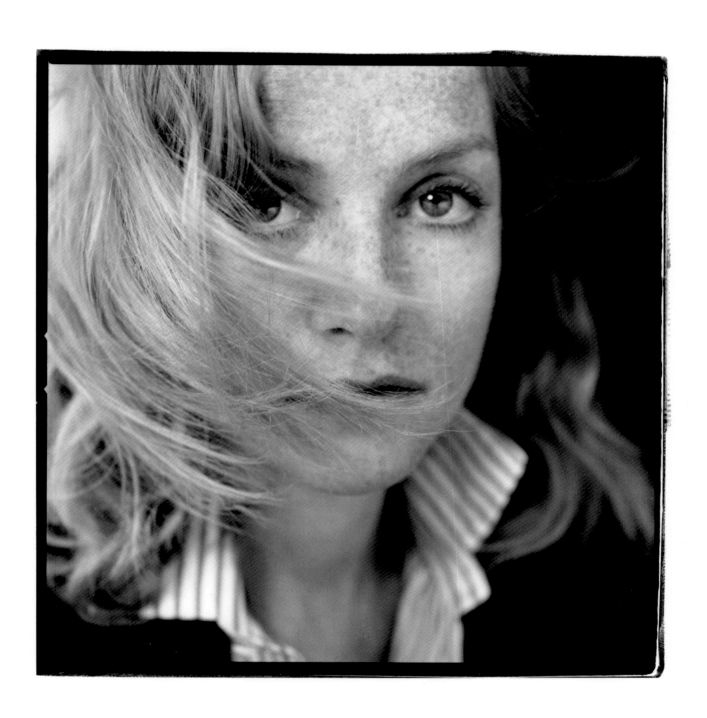

SYLVIA PLACHY, *1986*

61

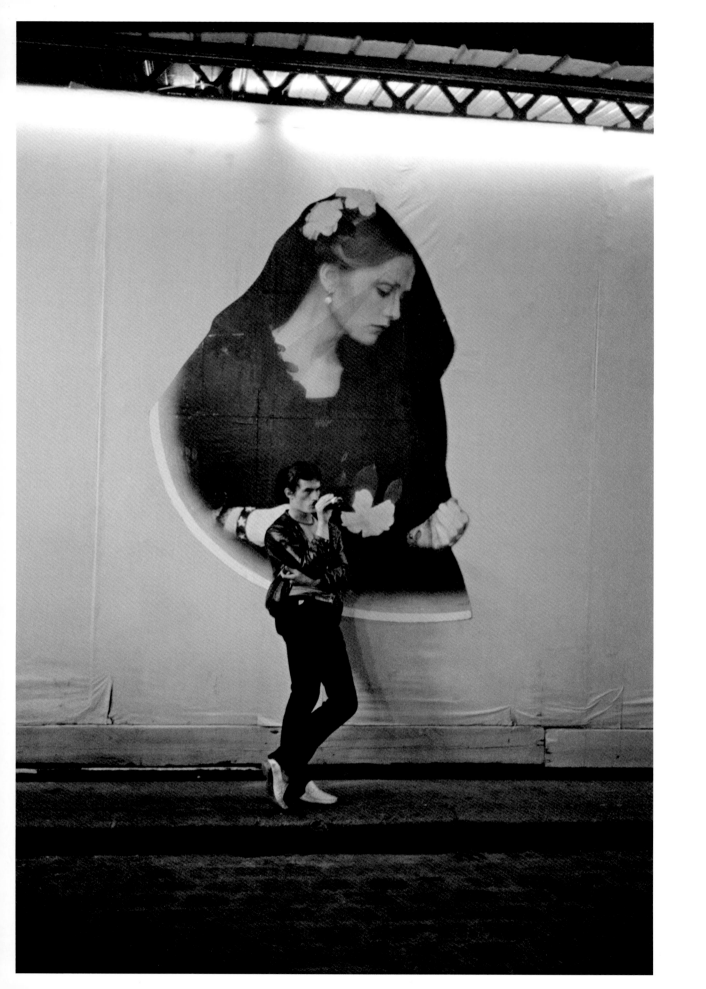

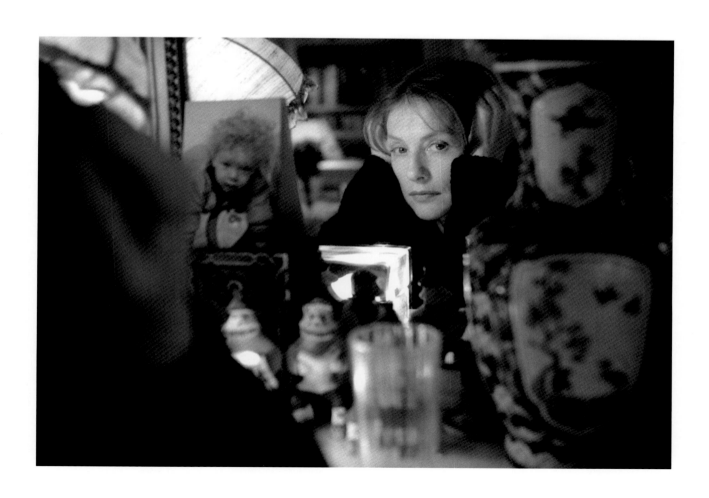

FERDINANDO SCIANNA, *1981, 2000*

63

WILLY RONIS,
1994

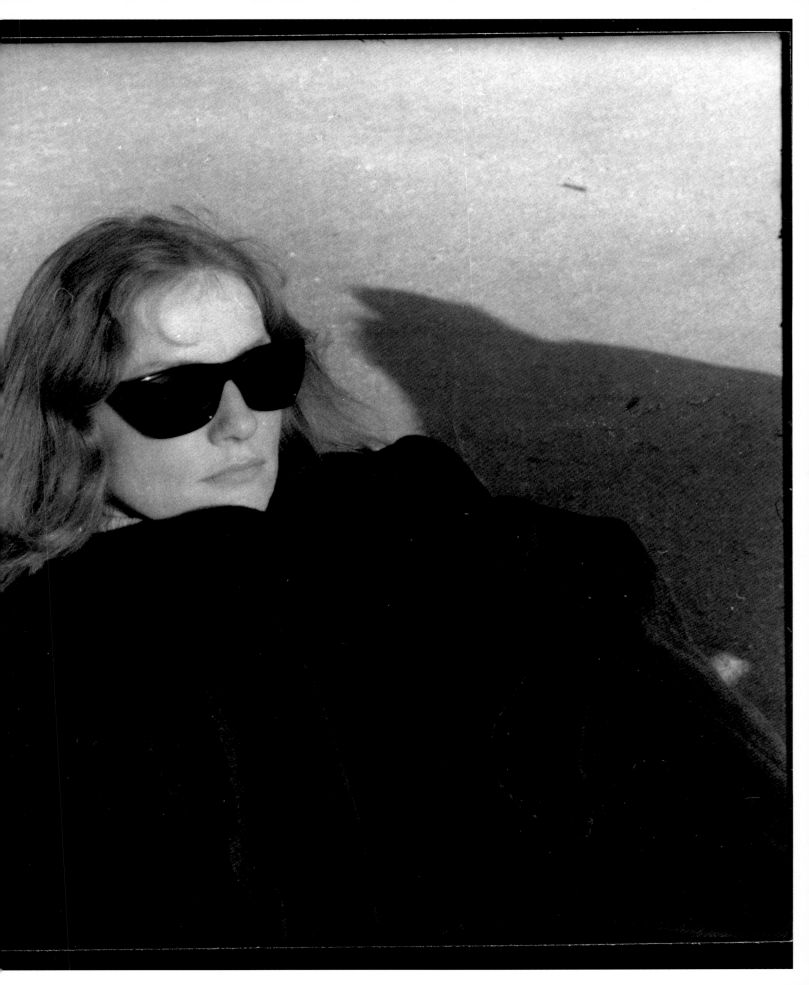

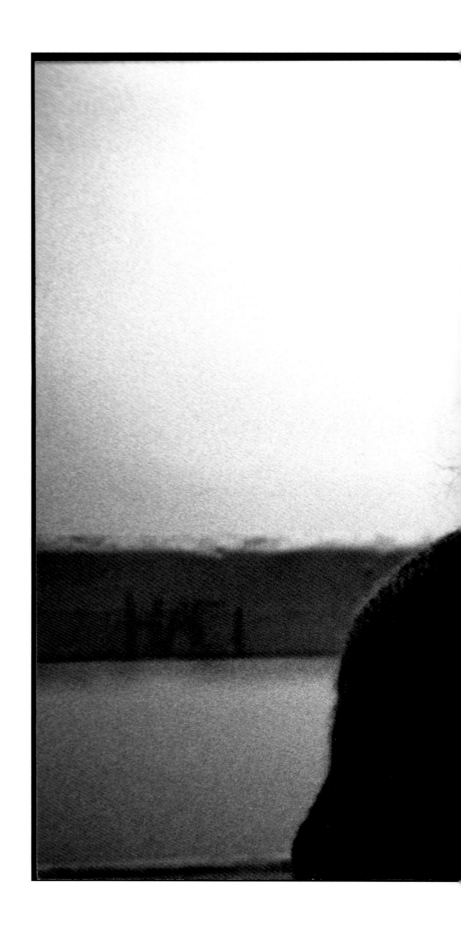

RONALD CHAMMAH, *1985*

66

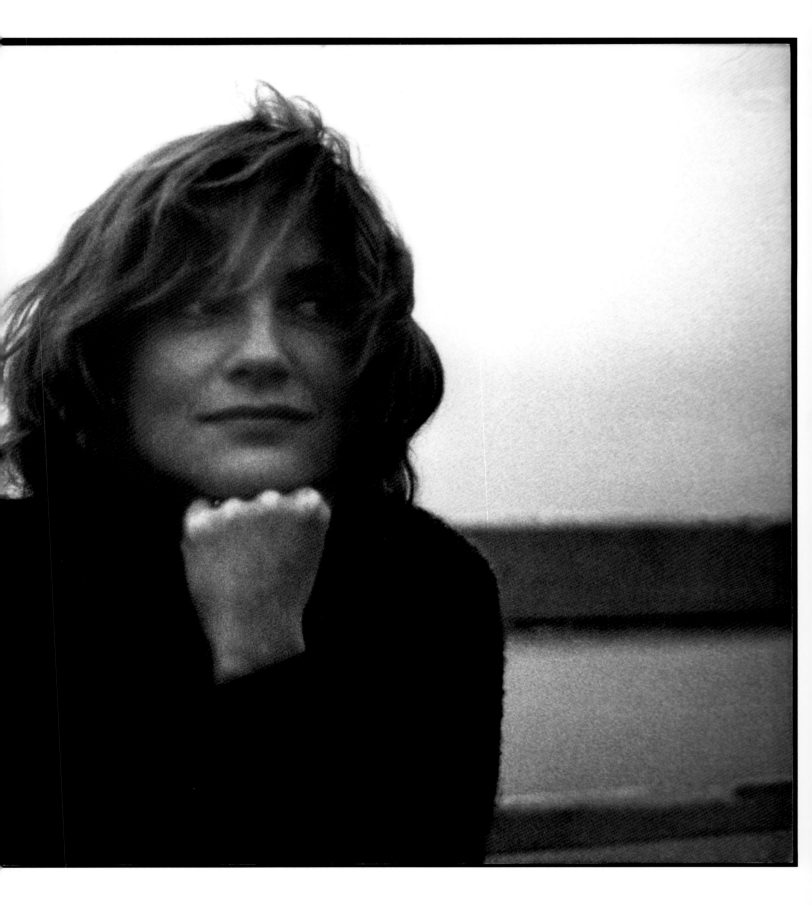

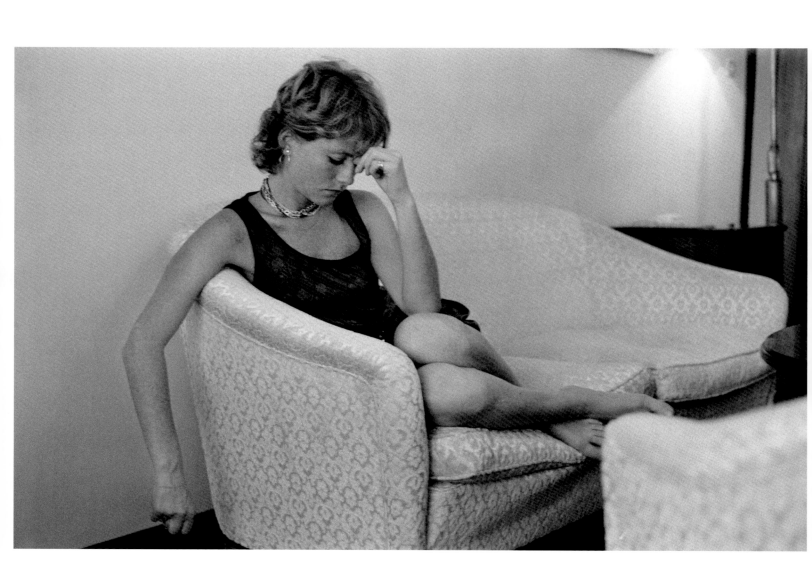

RAYMOND DEPARDON, *1982*

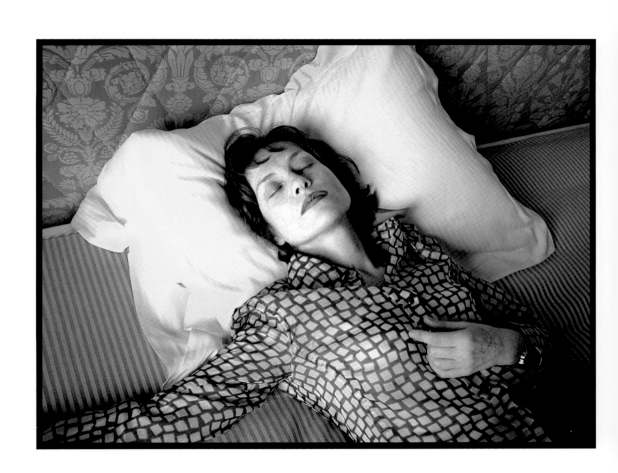

RICHARD DUMAS, *2000*

69

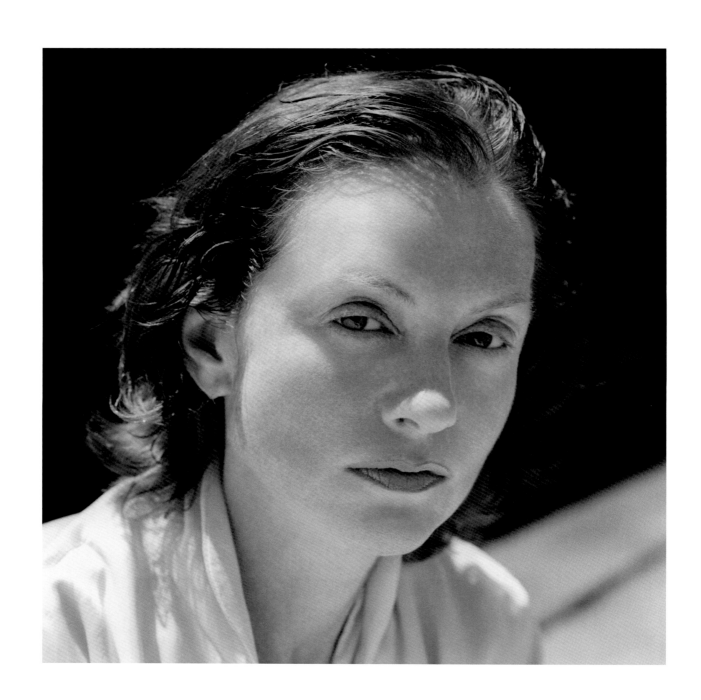

WILLIAM LAXTON. *2000*

70

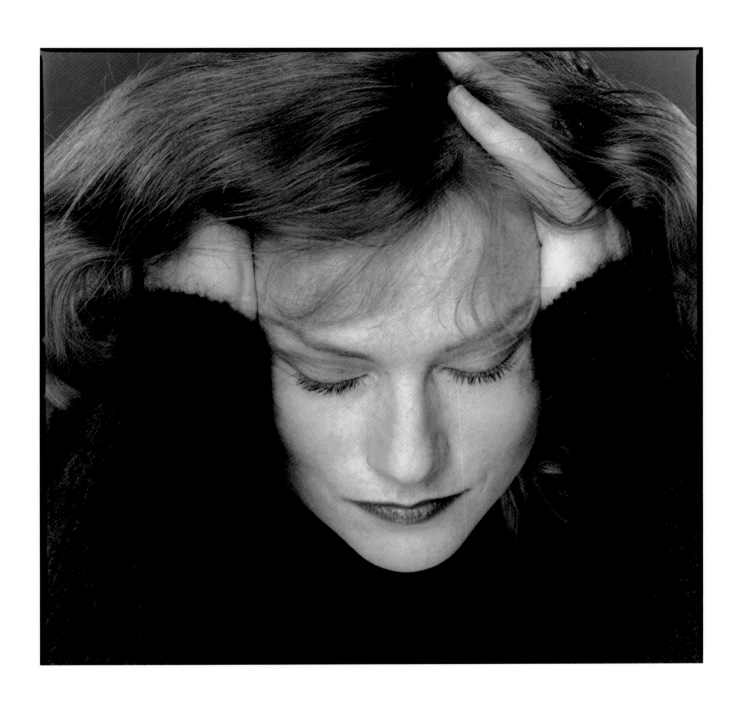

ROBIN HOLLAND, *1994*

71

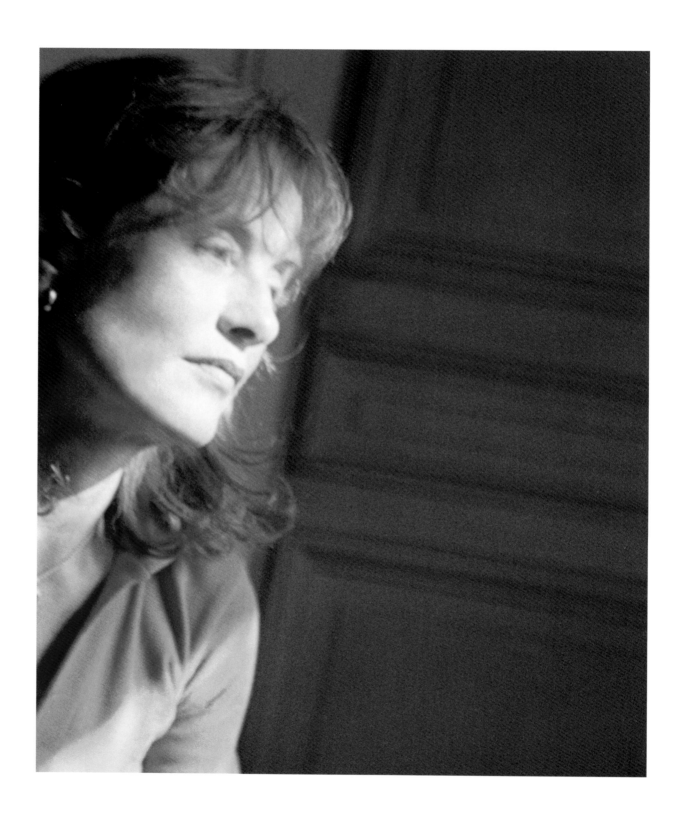

LUCIEN HERVÉ. *2003*

72

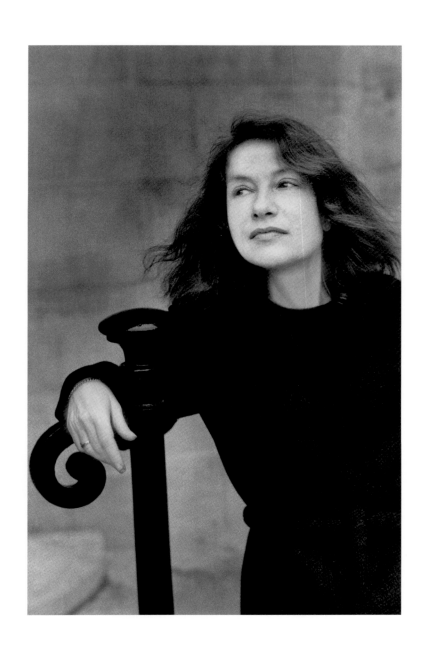

RALPH GIBSON, *2002*

73

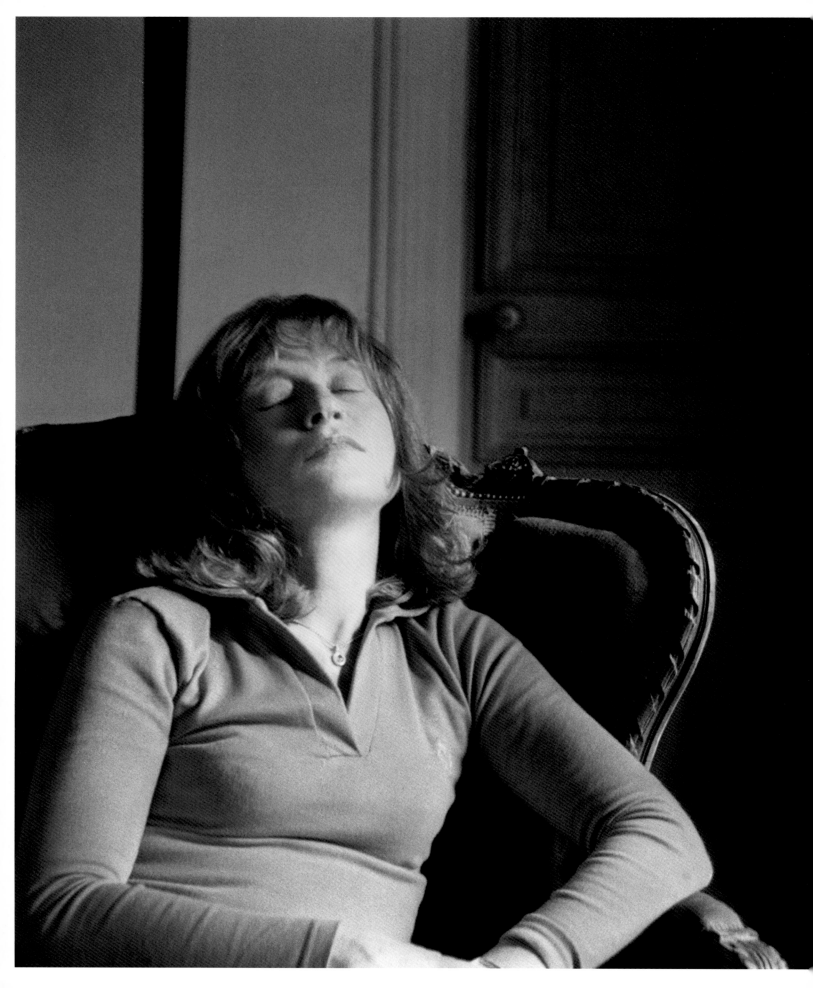

LUCIEN HERVÉ,
2003

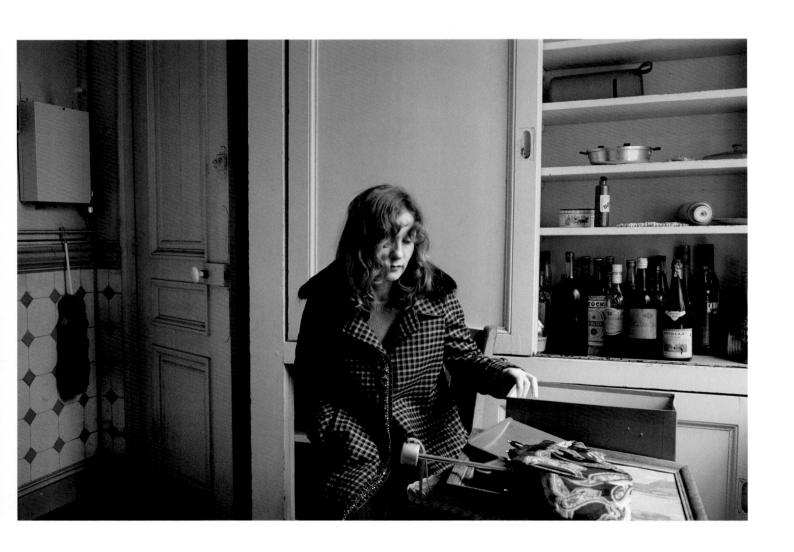

LISE SARFATI, *2004*

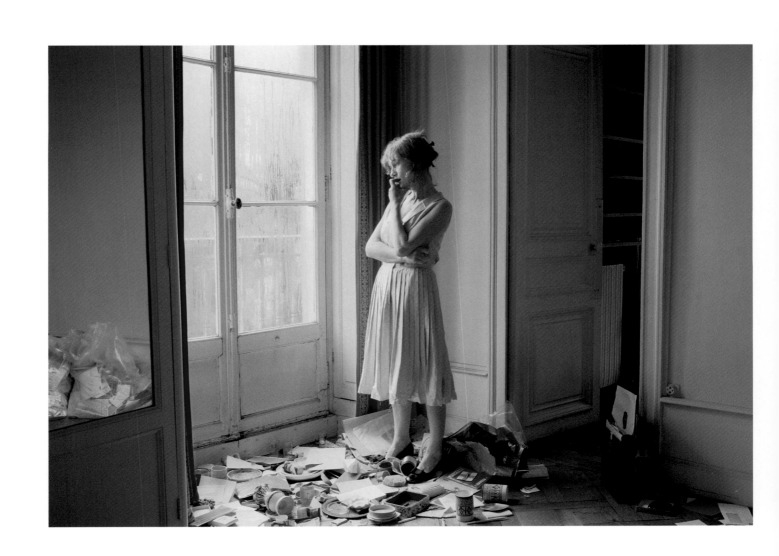

LISE SARFATI, *2004*

77

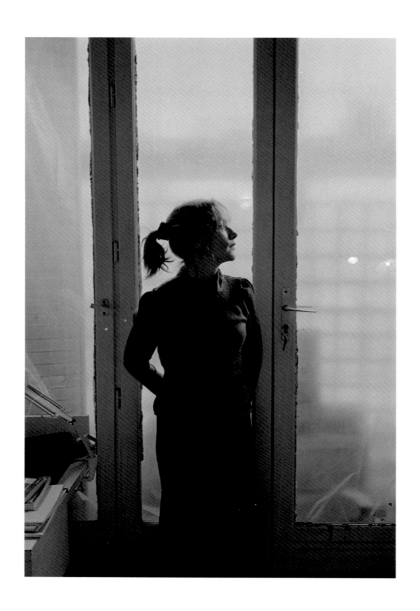

ELLIOTT ERWITT, *2002*
GUEORGUI PINKHASSOV, *2002*

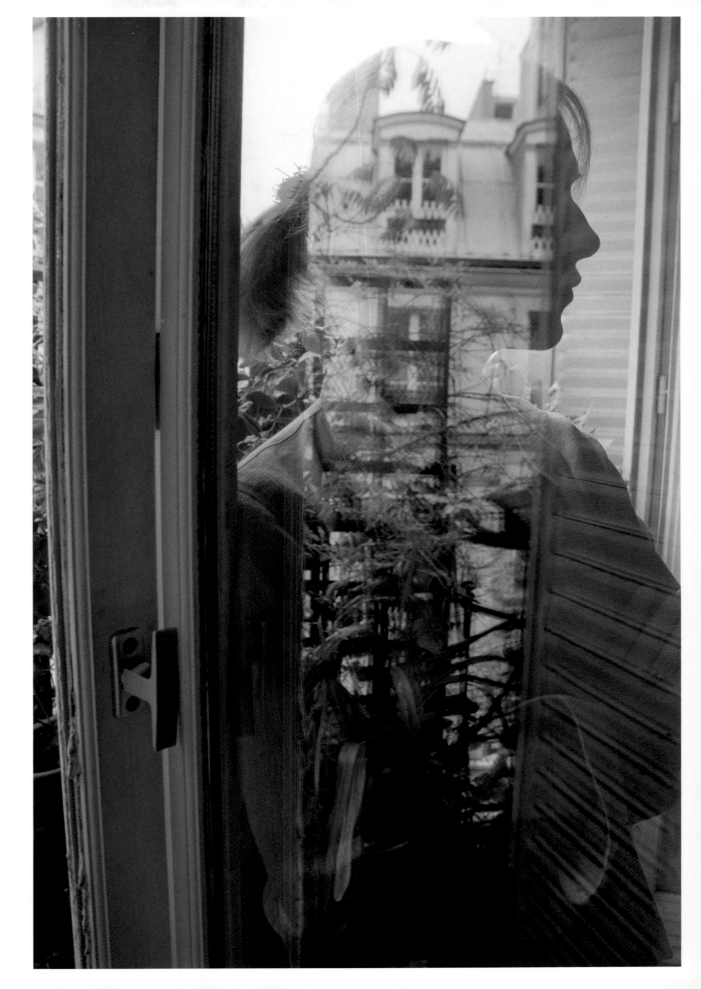

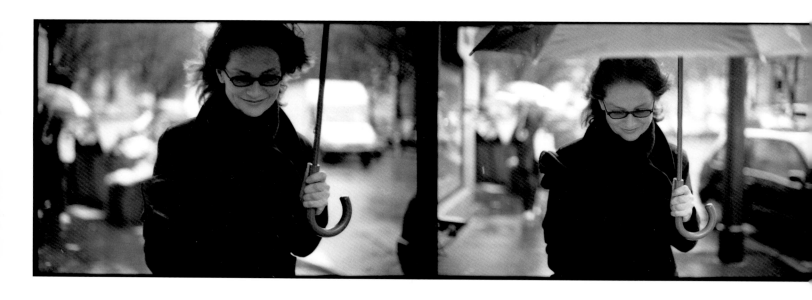

BERNARD PLOSSU. *2002*

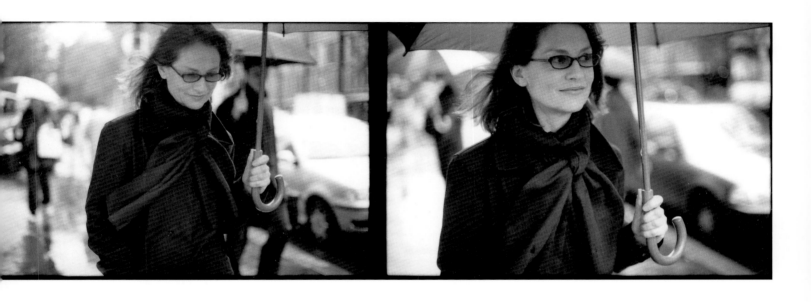

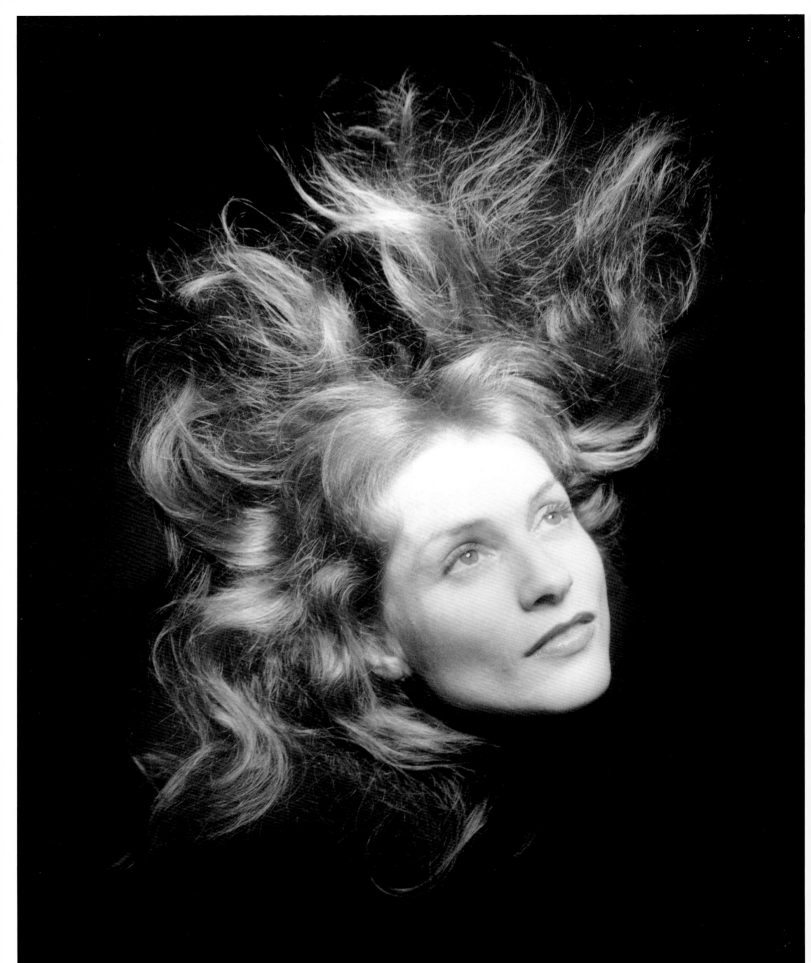

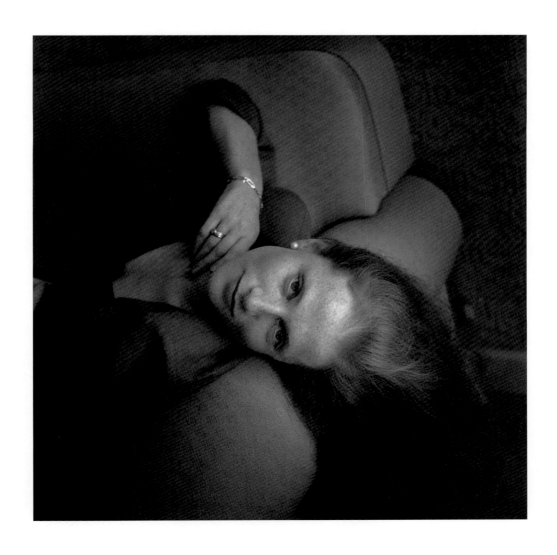

JEAN-CHRISTIAN BOURCART, *1989*
HUGUES DE WURSTEMBERGER, *1988*

83

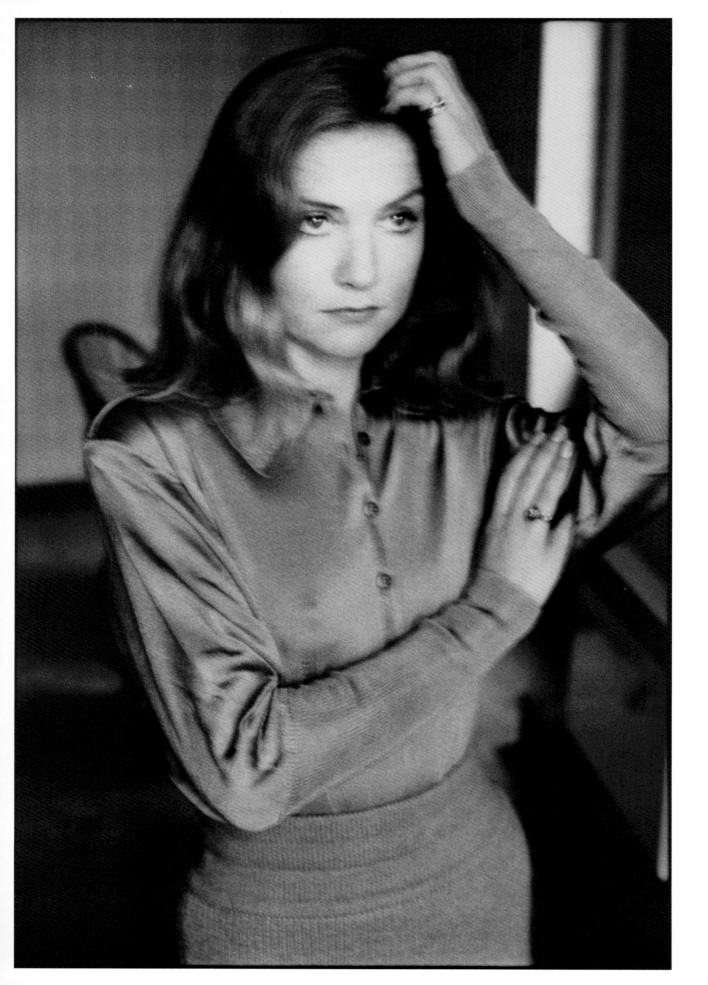

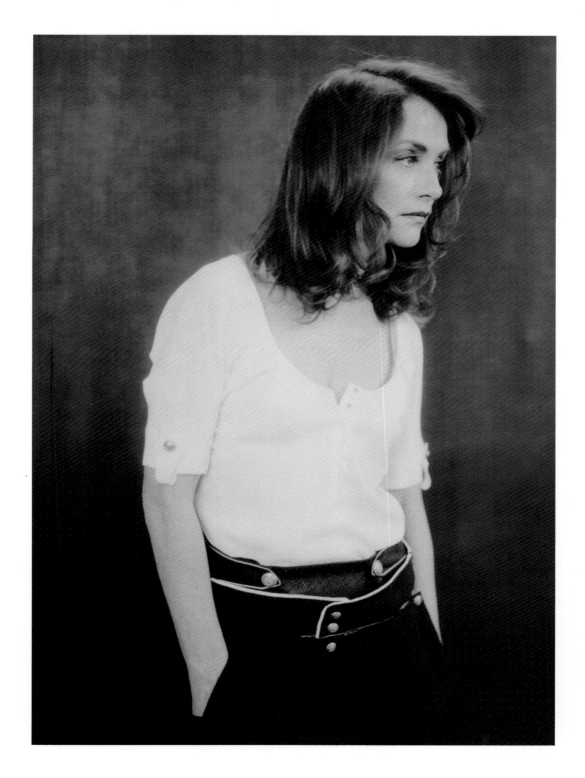

PETE MOSS, *1987*
PAOLO ROVERSI, *2005*

ANONYMOUS, *1968*

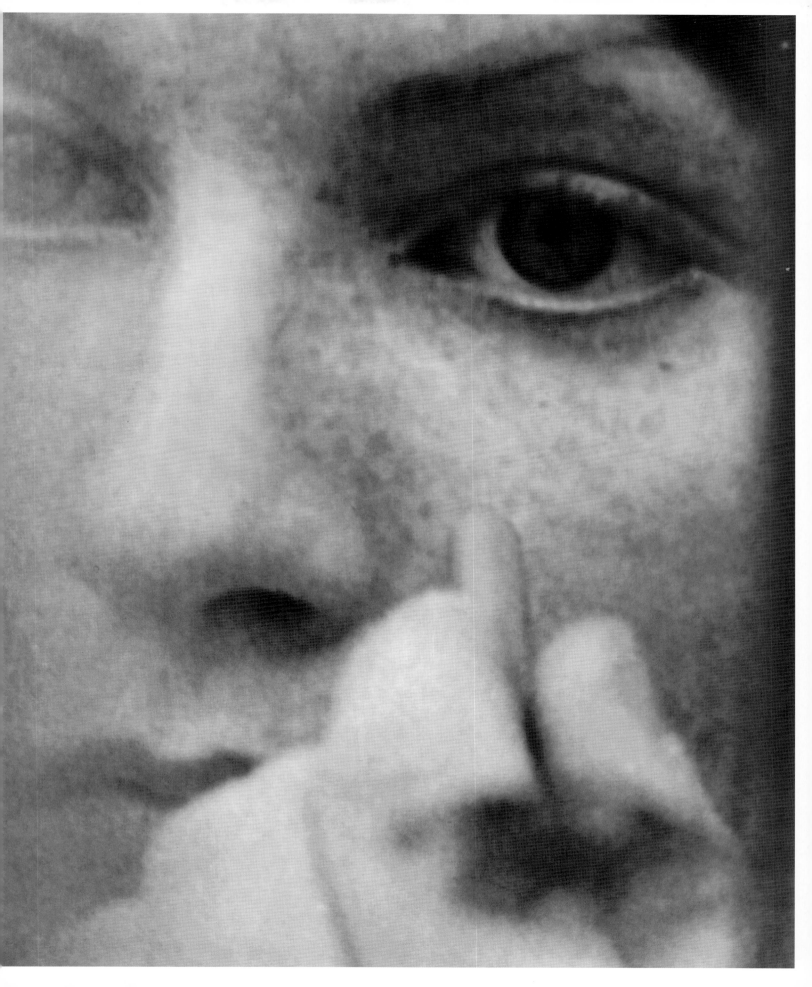

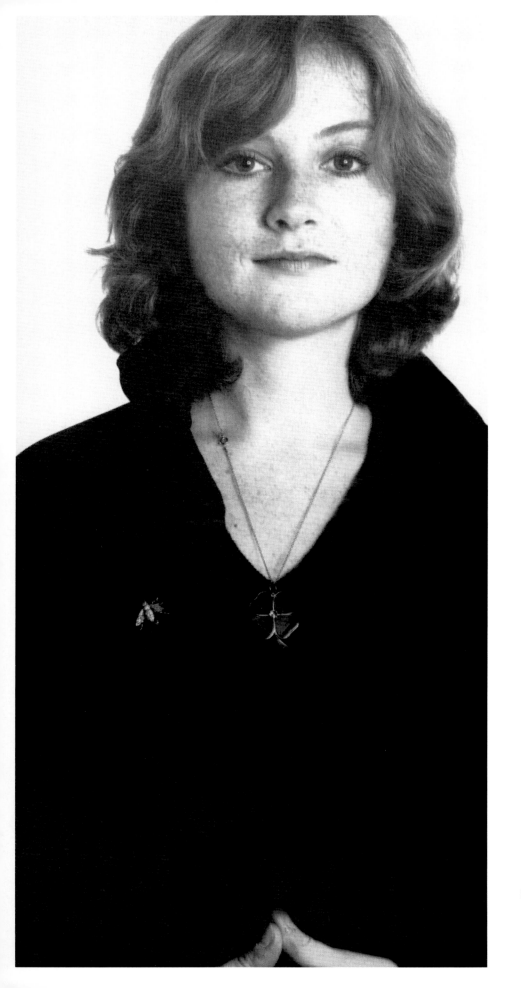

RICHARD AVEDON, *1978, 1980*

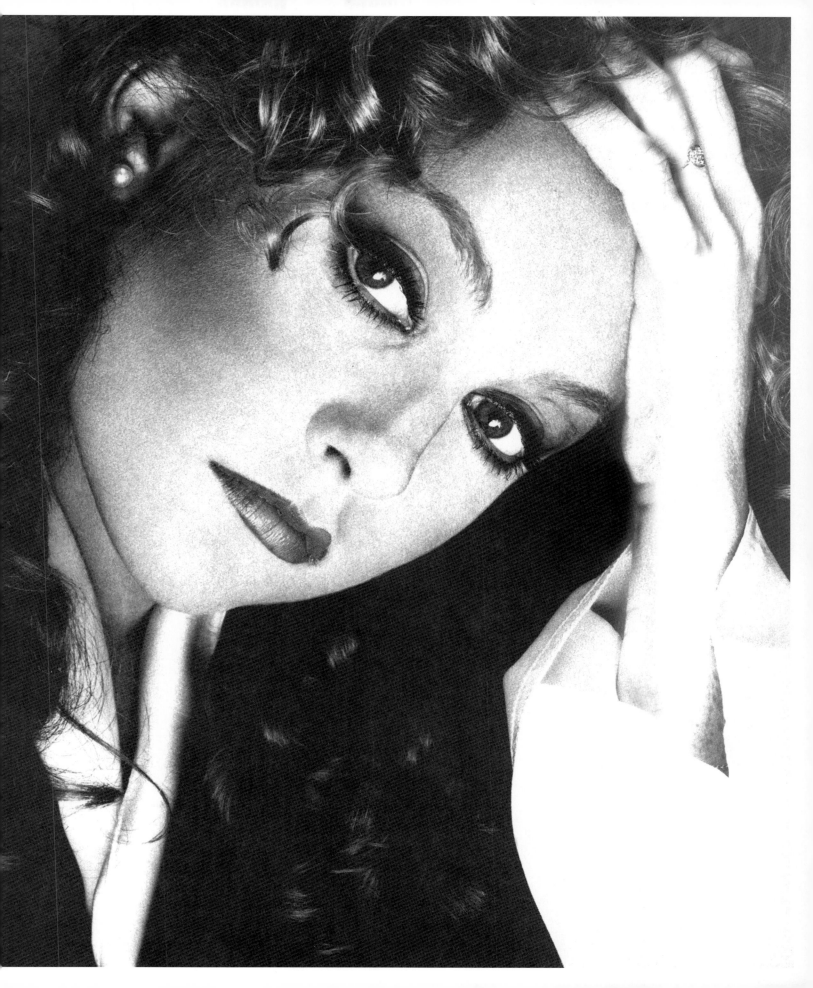

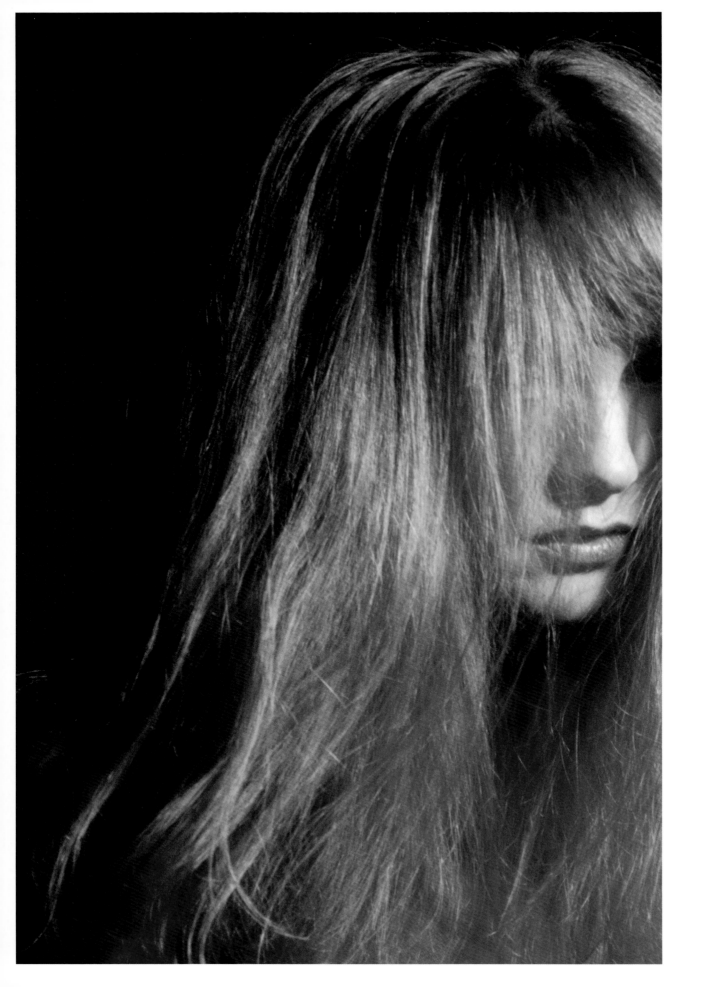

GUY
BOURDIN.
1989

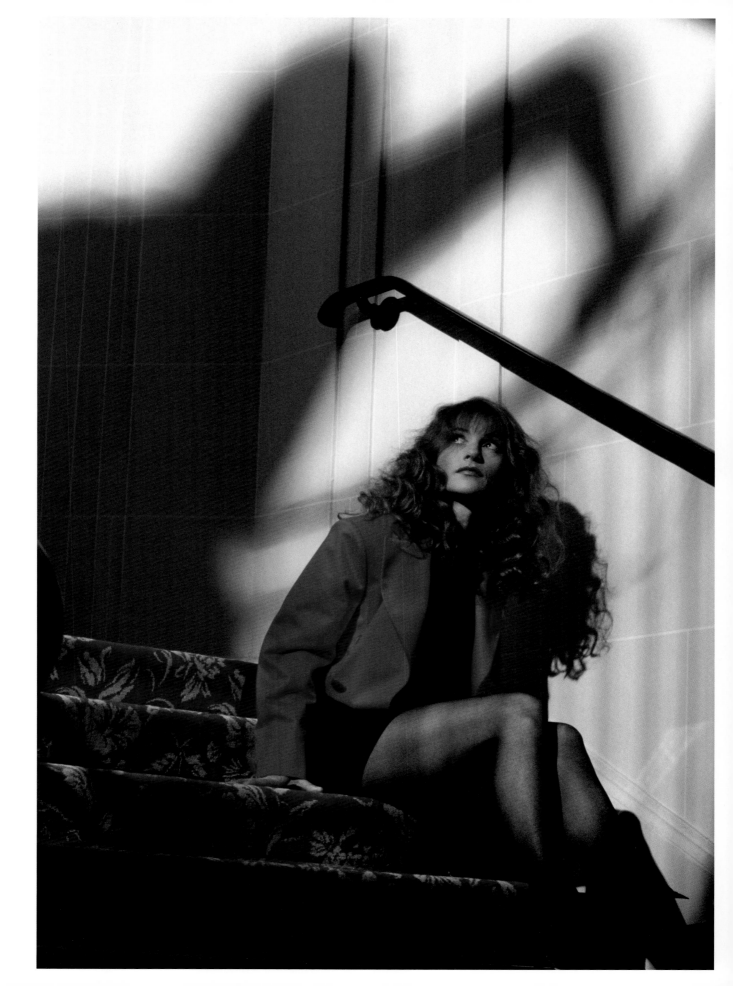

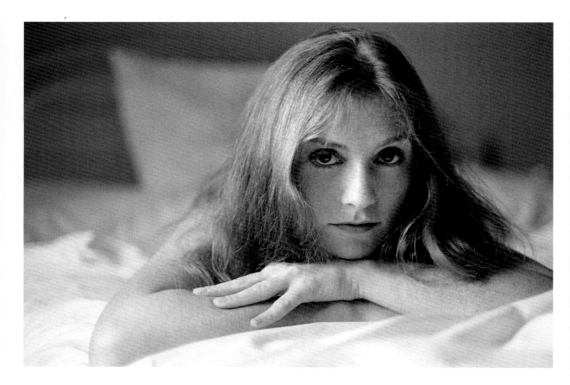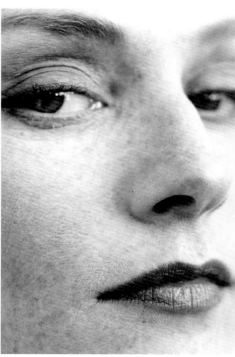

BRIGITTE LACOMBE. *1988, 1991, 1997*

92

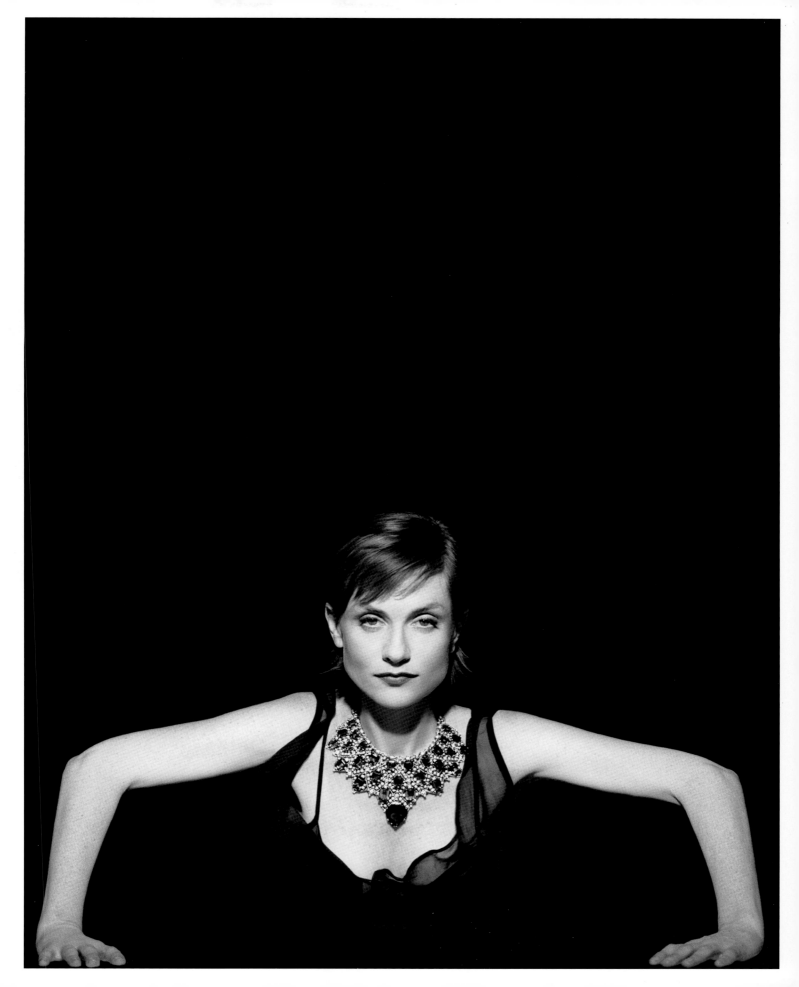

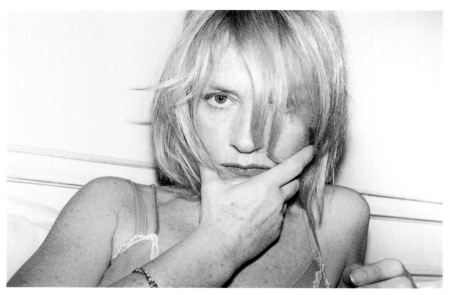

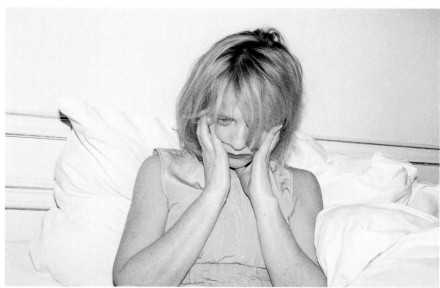

JUERGEN TELLER, *2001*

96

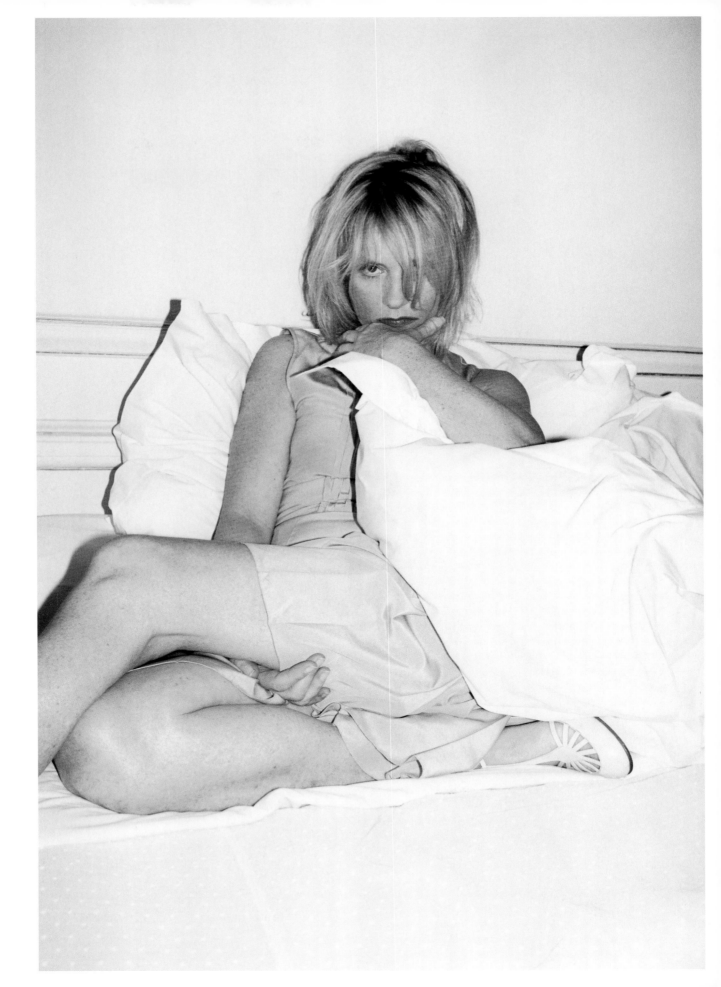

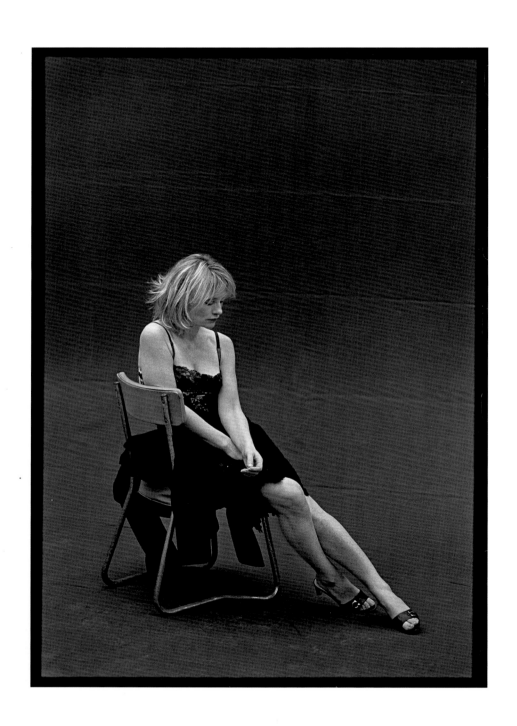

PETER LINDBERGH, *2002*

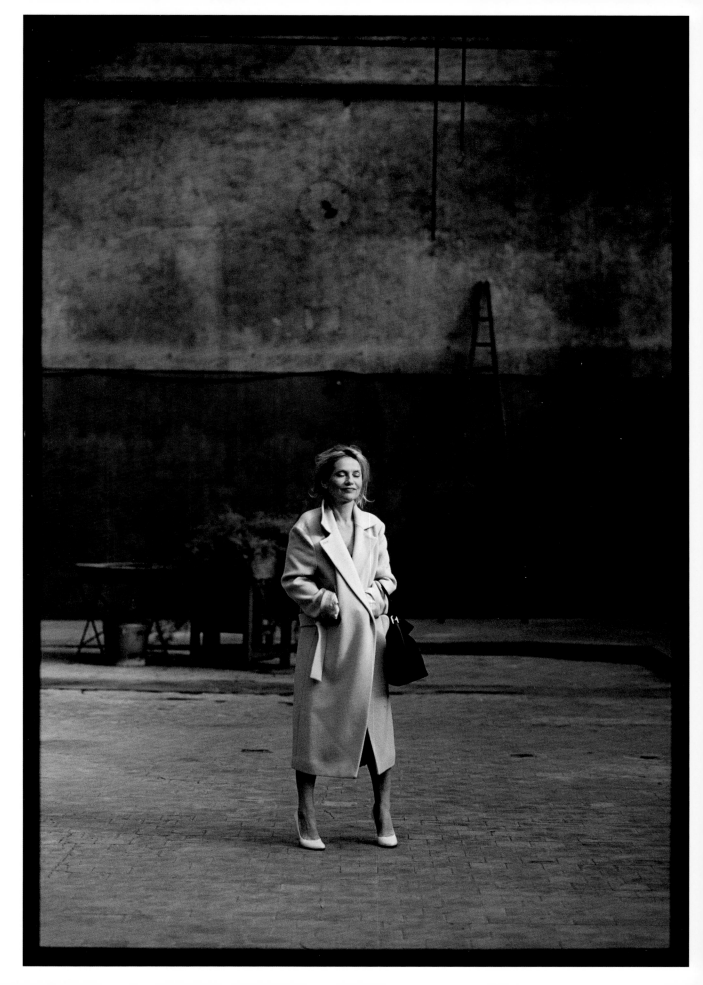

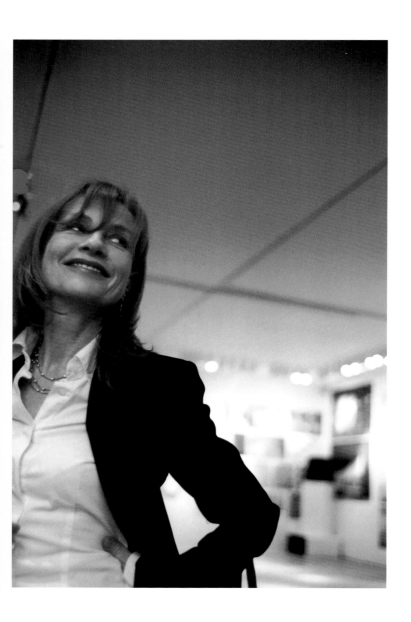

WILLIAM EGGLESTON, *2004*
PETER LINDBERGH, *2001*

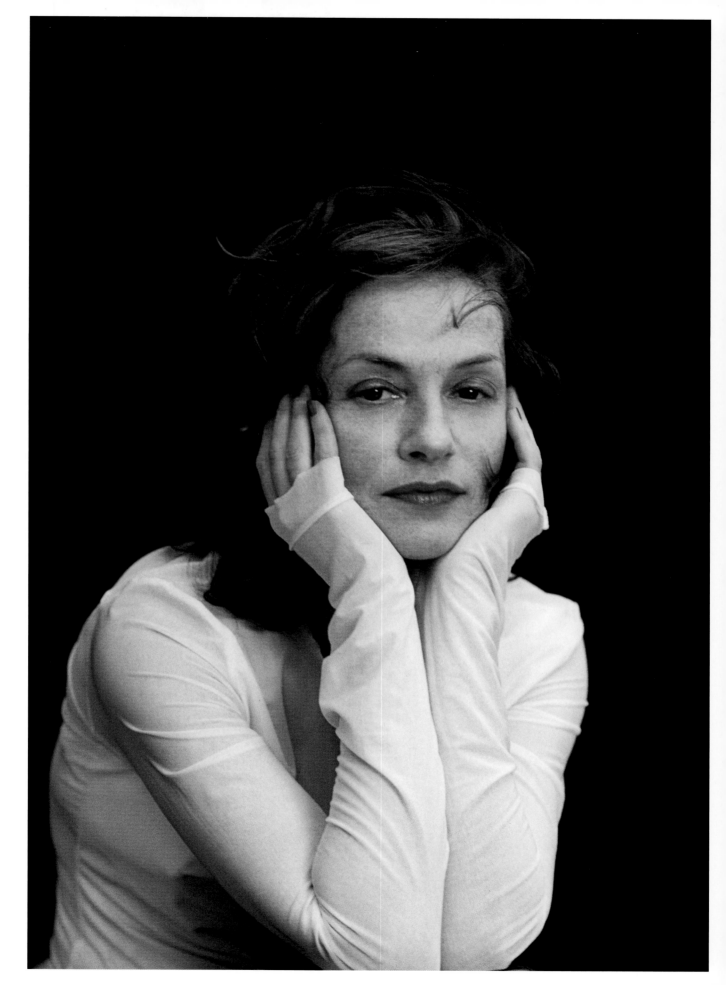

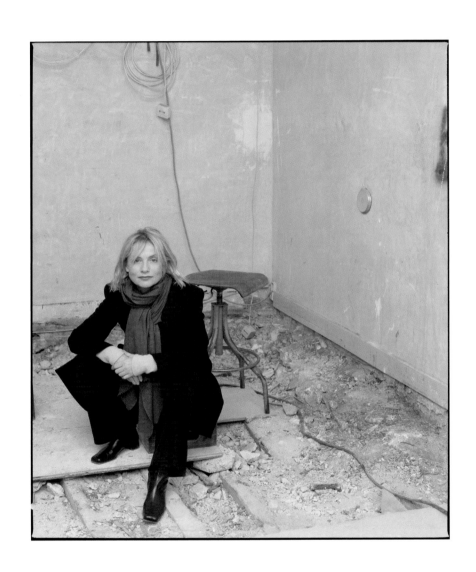

ANNIE LEIBOVITZ, *2002*

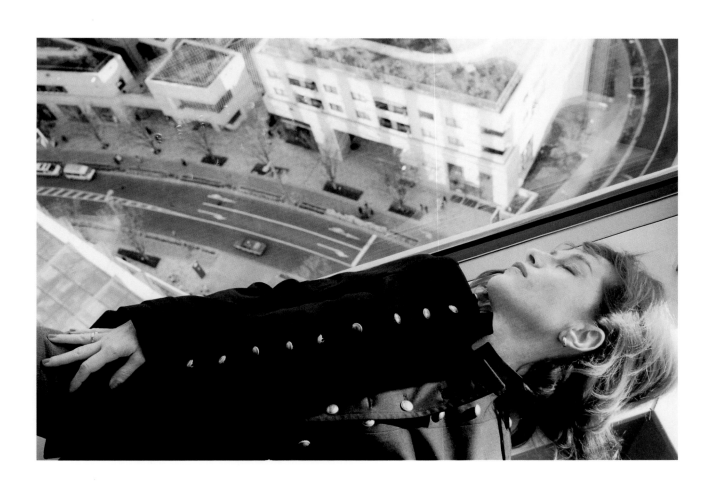

CLAUDINE DOURY, *2004*

101

MICHEL COMTE, *1989*

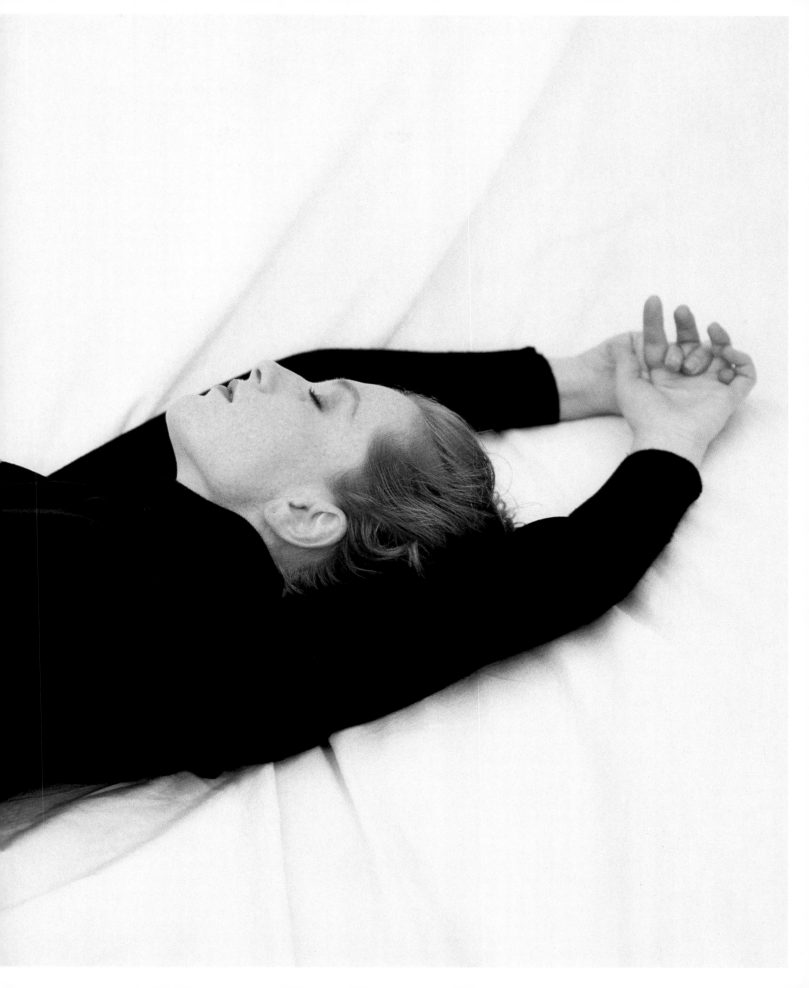

NICK KNIGHT. *1989*

104

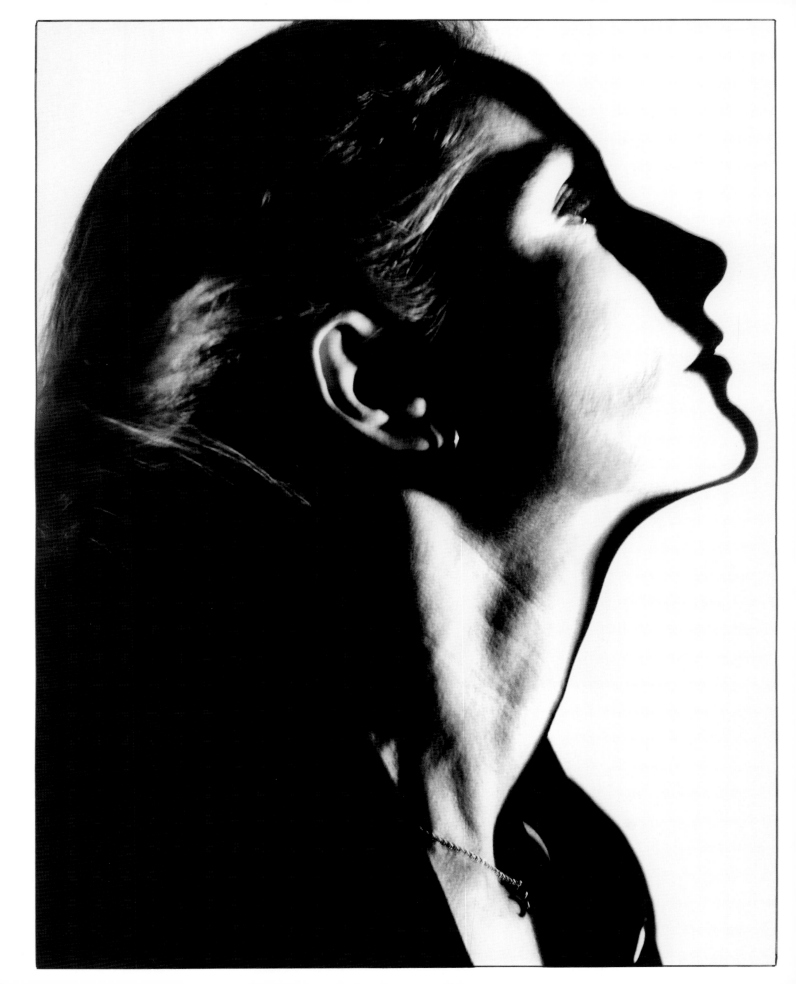

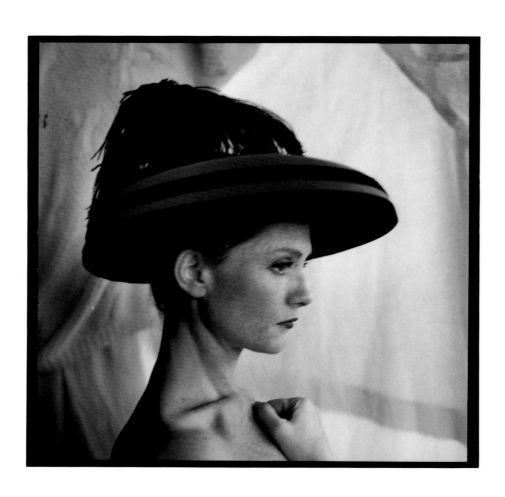

SYLVIA PLACHY, *1986*
DOUGLAS KIRKLAND, *1985*
106

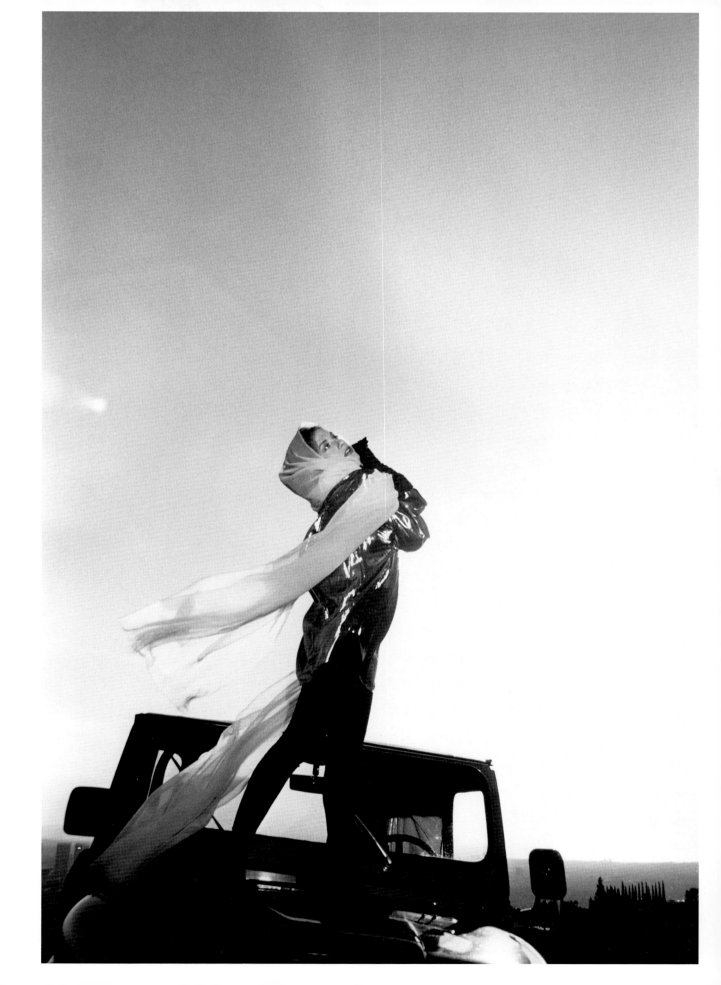

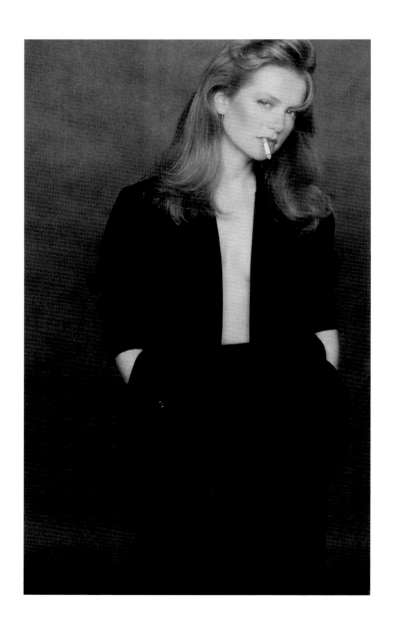

PATRICK DEMARCHELIER, *1981*
PAOLO ROVERSI, *2005*

108

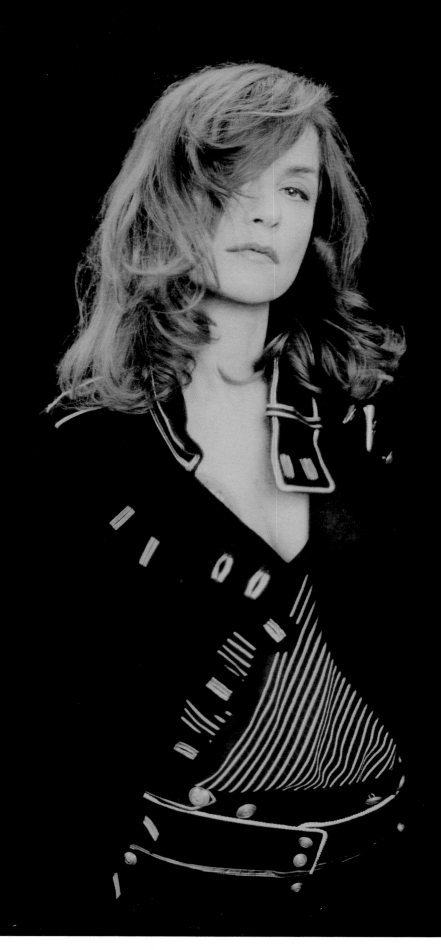

PAOLO ROVERSI, *1985*

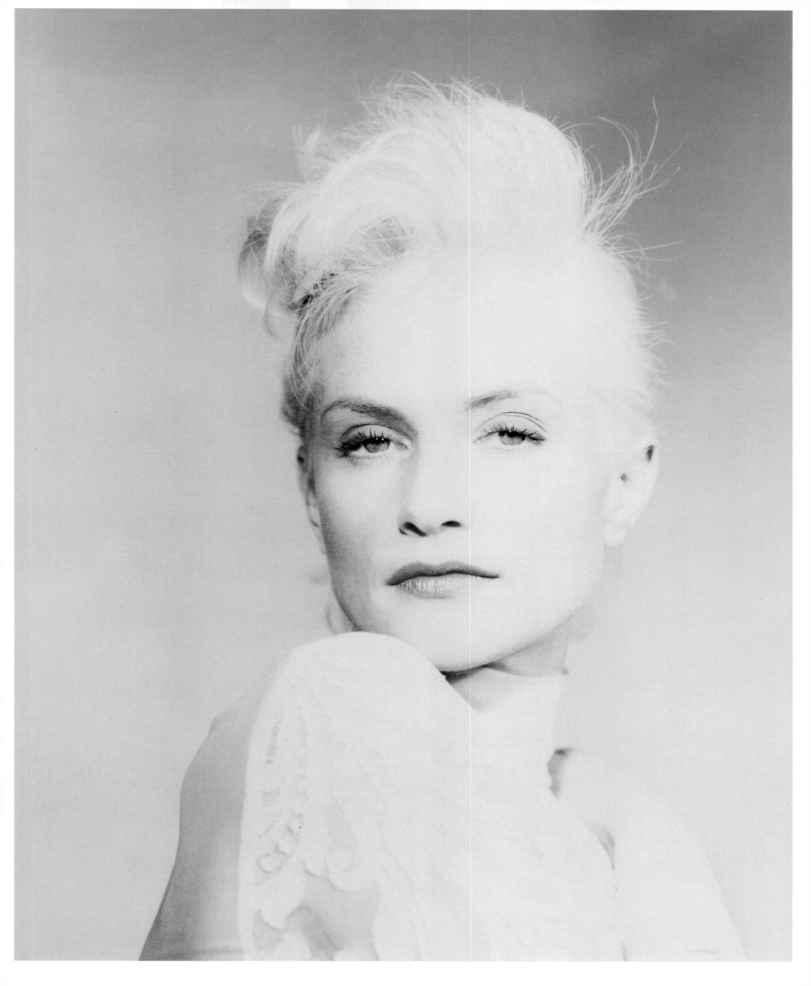

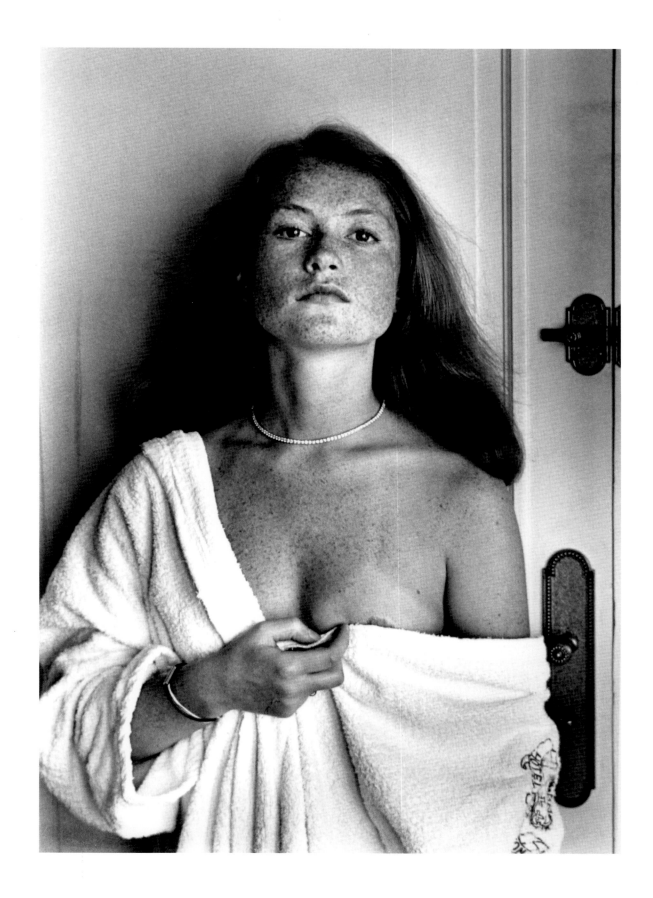

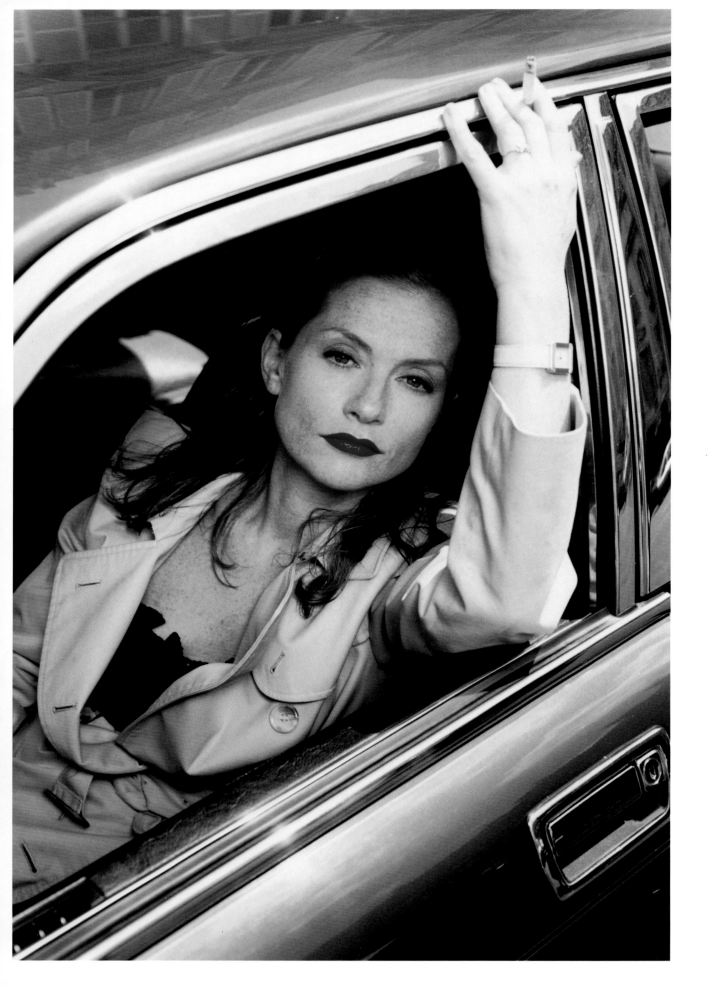

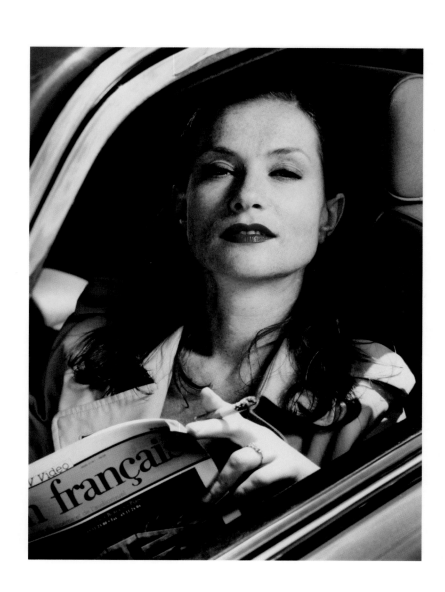

HELMUT NEWTON, *1993*

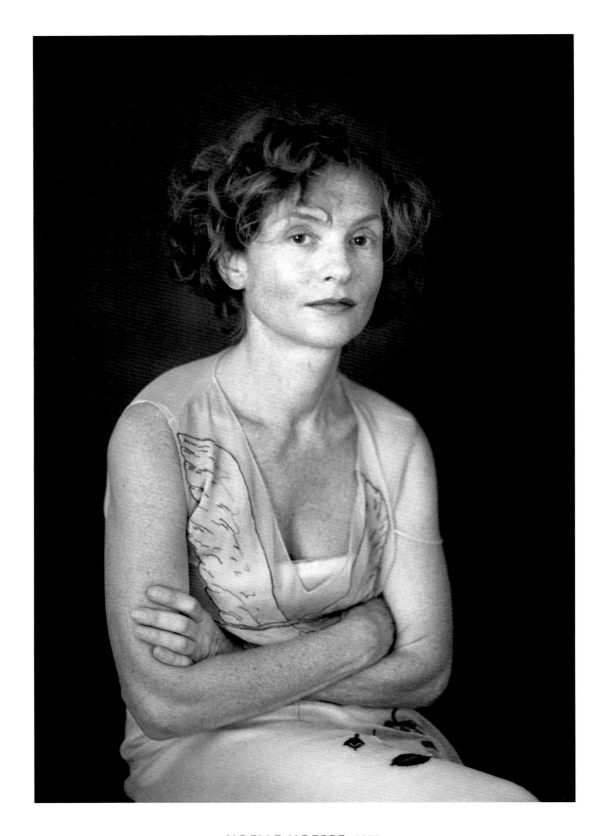

NOELLE HOEPPE. *1998*

116

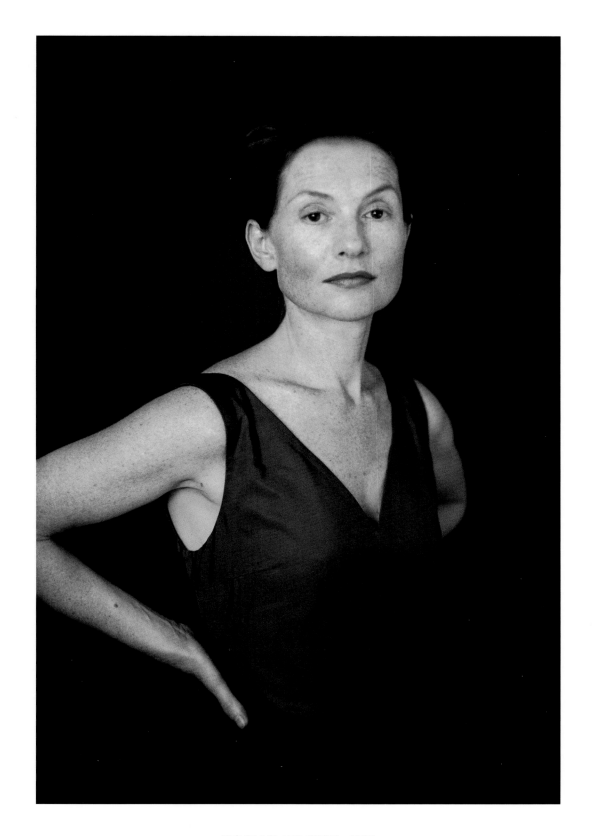

NOELLE HOEPPE, *1998*

117

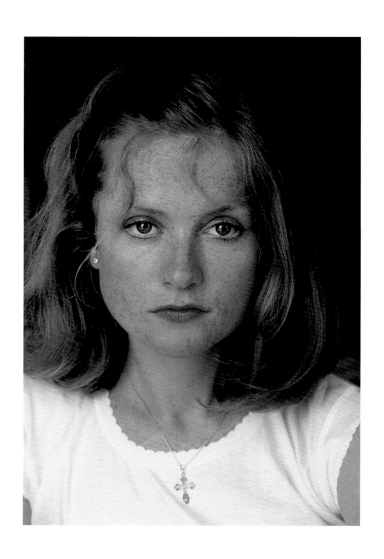

MARIE-LAURE DE DECKER, *1981*
JEANLOUP SIEFF, *1985*
118

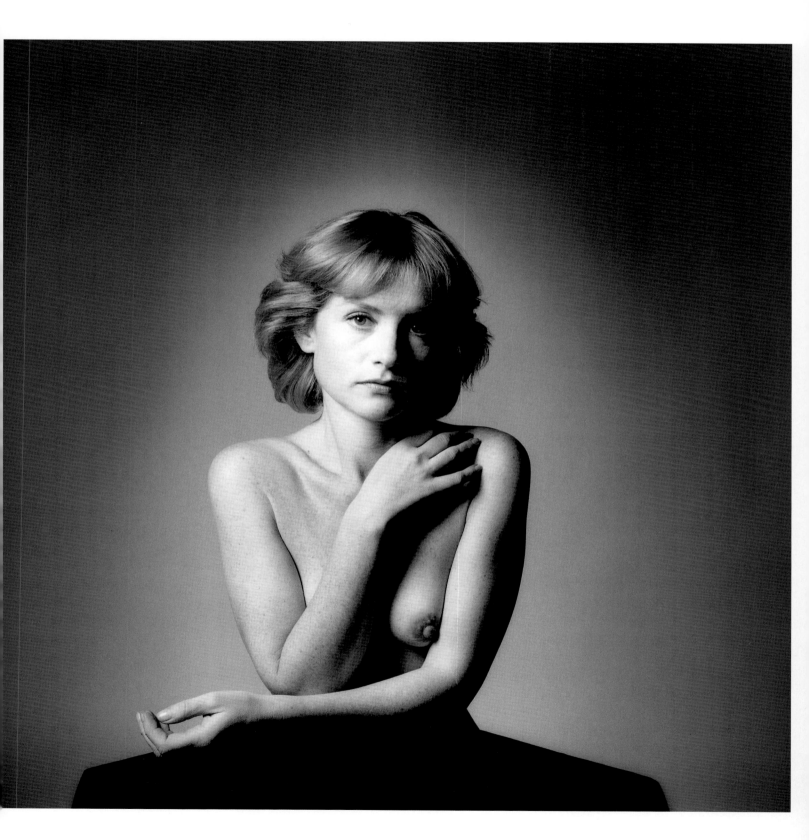

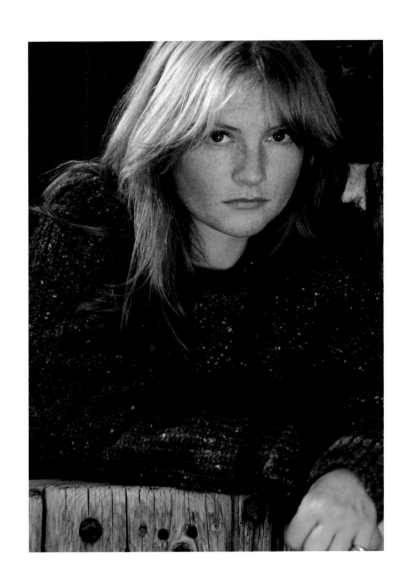

HERB RITTS, *1980*
PÉNÉLOPE CHAUVELOT, *1973*

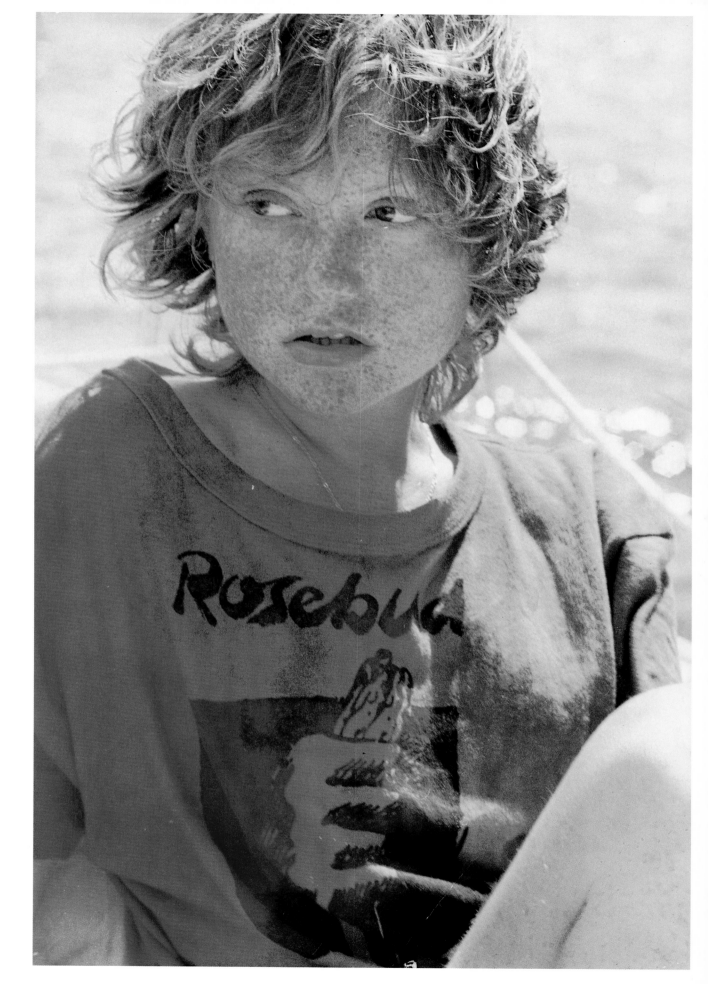

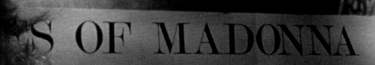

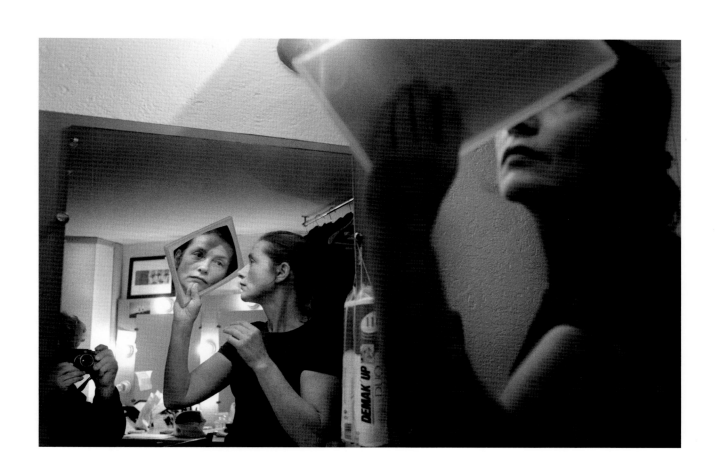

LEONARD FREED, *1992*
GUY LE QUERREC, *2002*

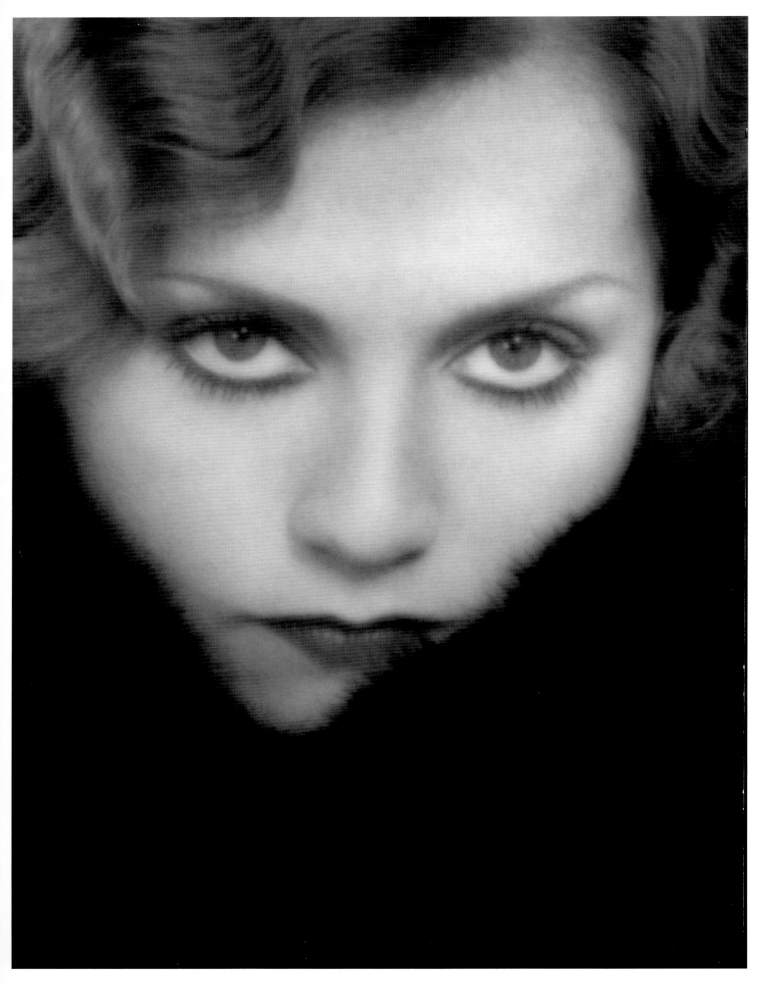

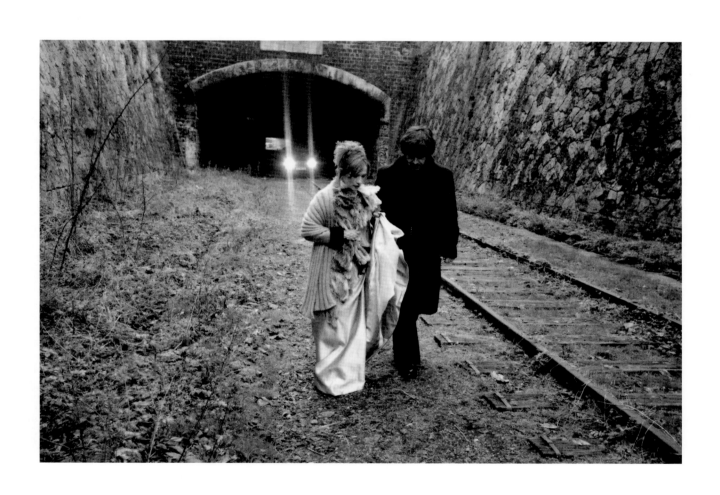

ROGER CORBEAU, *1978*
FRANK HORVAT, *2001*

125

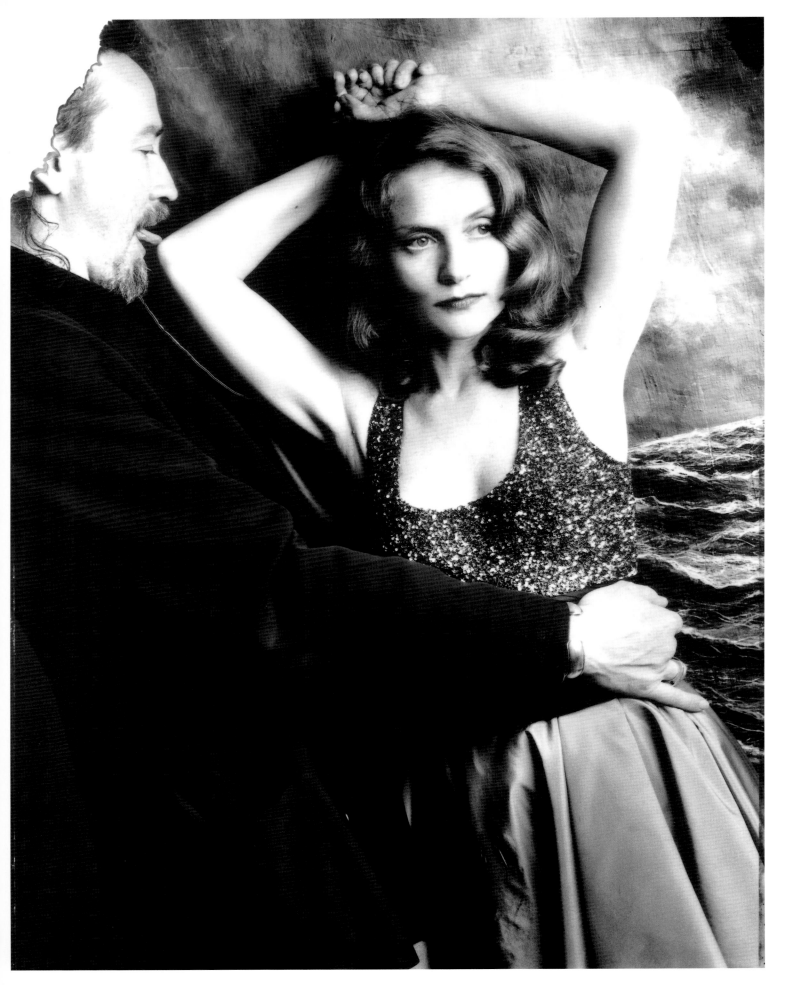

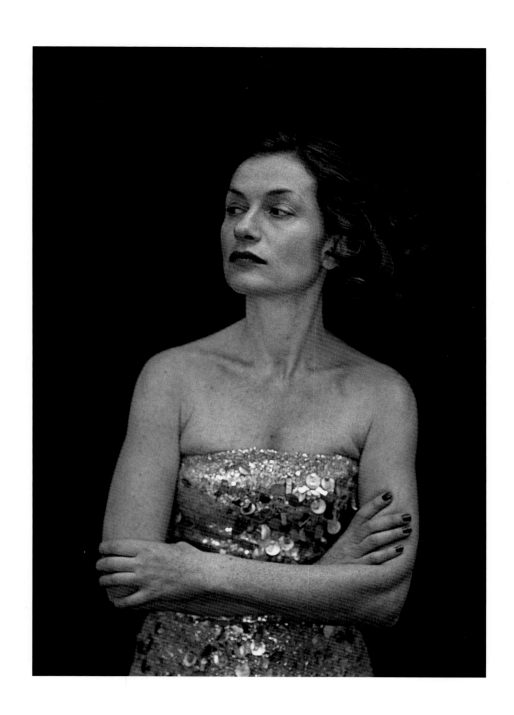

ARNAUD BAUMANN, *1991*
PETER LINDBERGH, *2001*

127

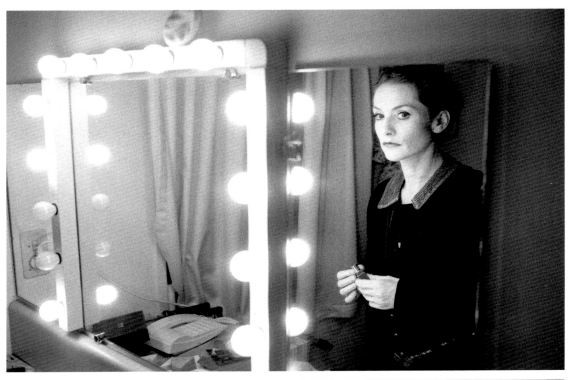

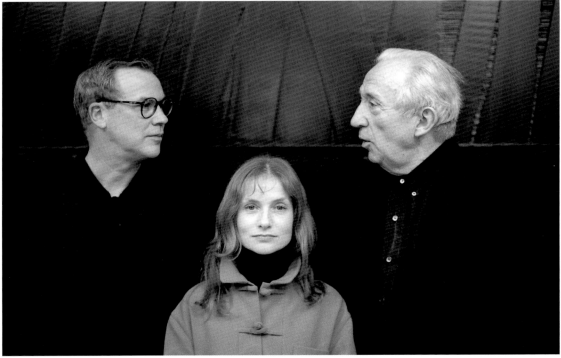

MICHEL VANDEN EECKHOUDT, *1993*
MARC RIBOUD, *1993*
JÉRÔME BRÉZILLON, *1998*

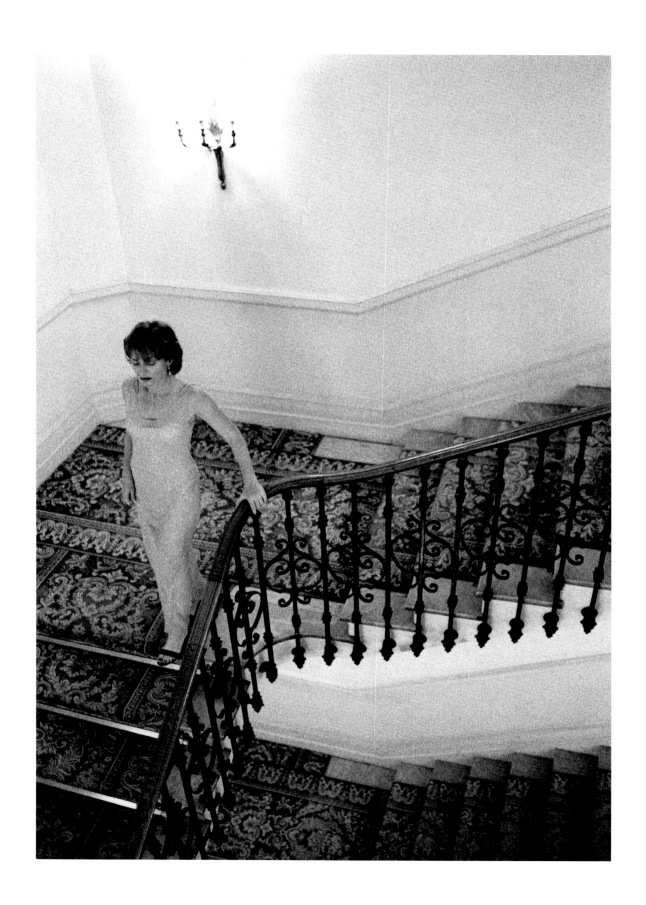

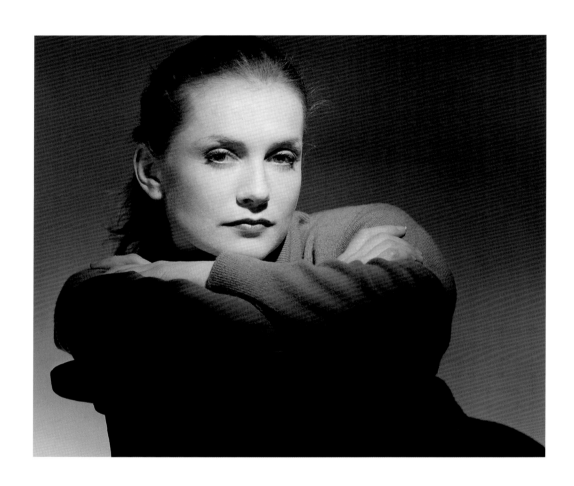

STUDIO HARCOURT, *1987*
LEN PRINCE, *1994*

130

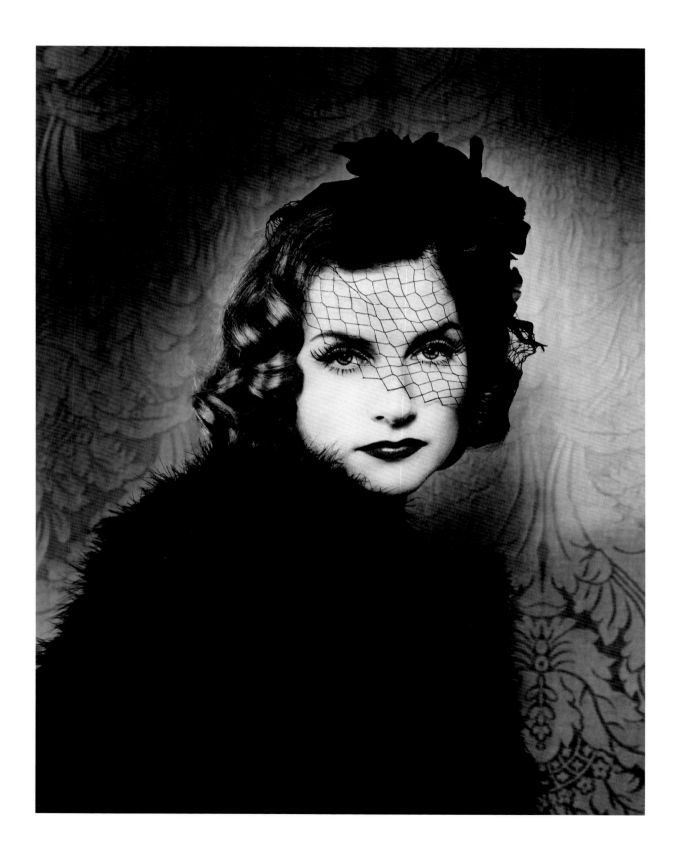

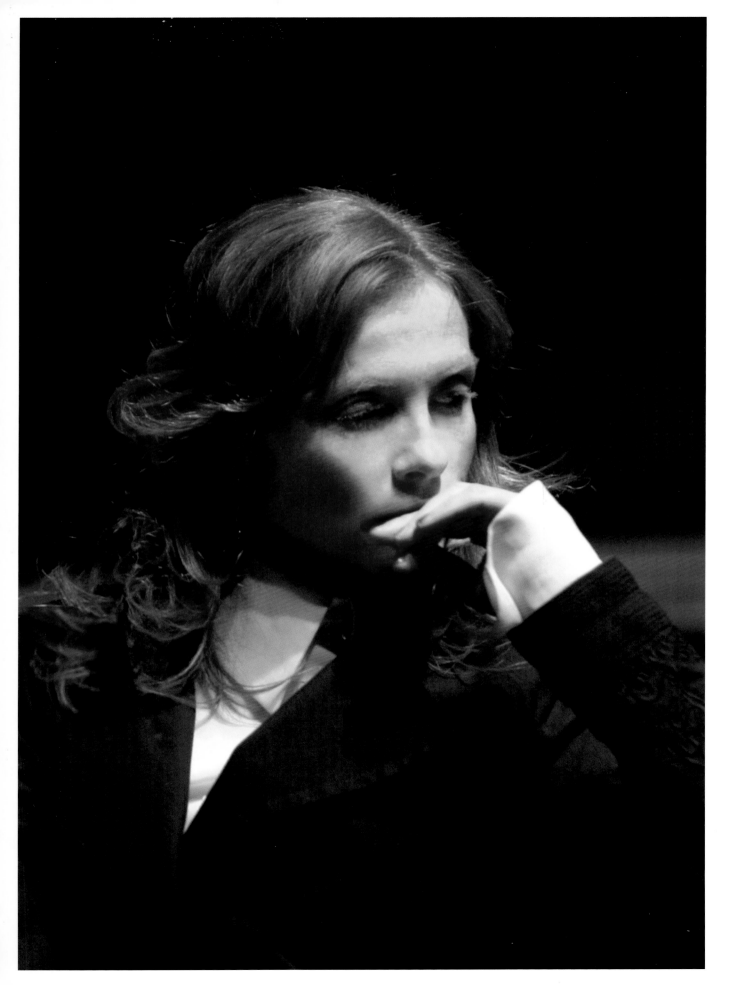

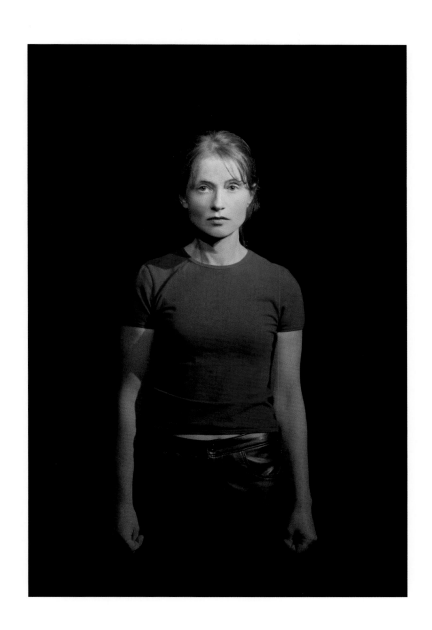

PASCAL VICTOR. *2004. 2002*

133

PASCAL VICTOR, *1993*

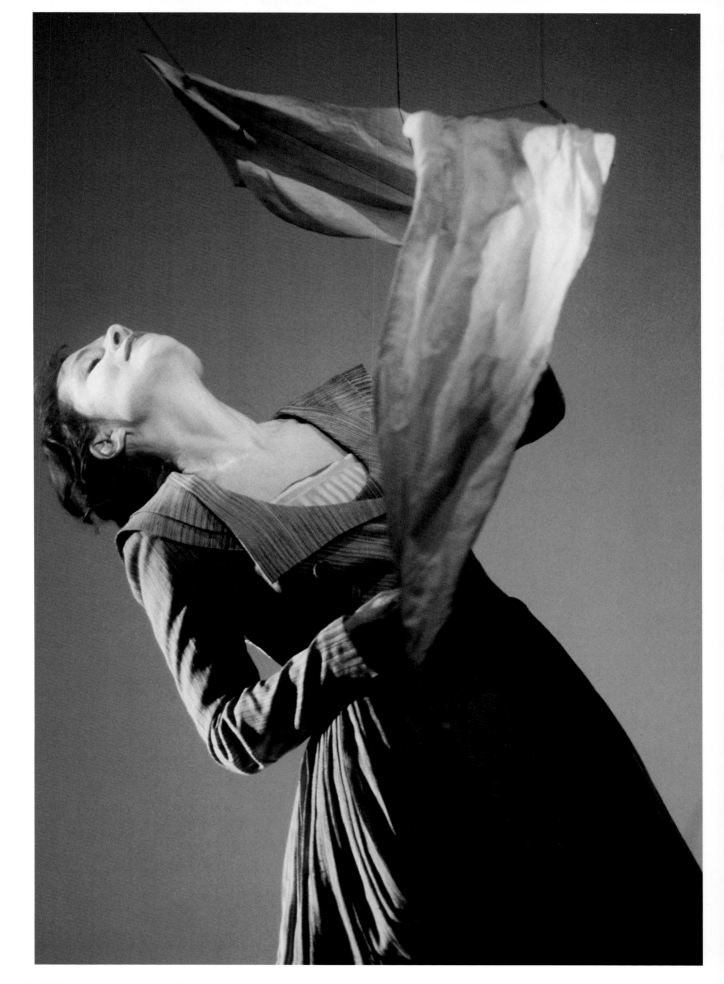

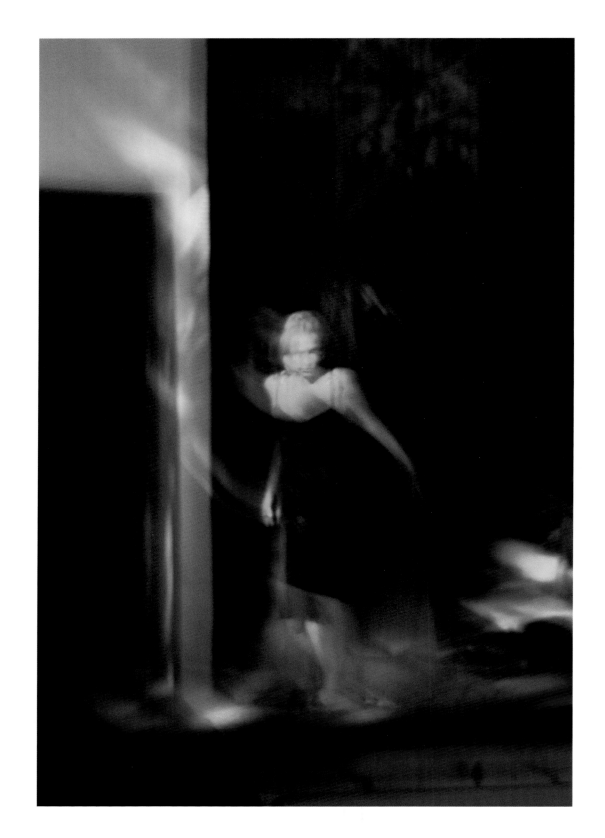

ANTOINE D'AGATA, 2003

136

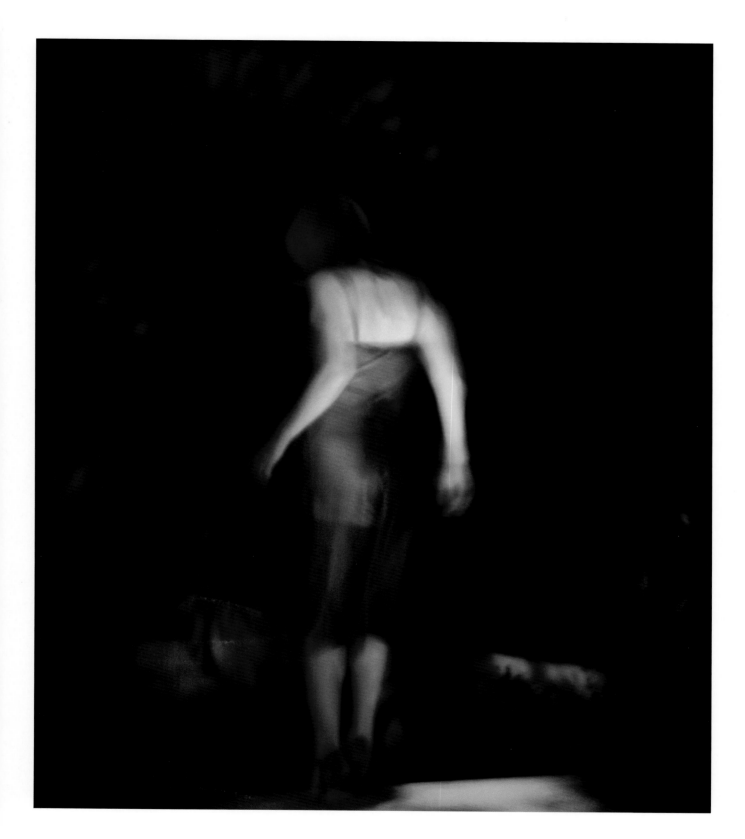

ANTOINE D'AGATA, *2003*

137

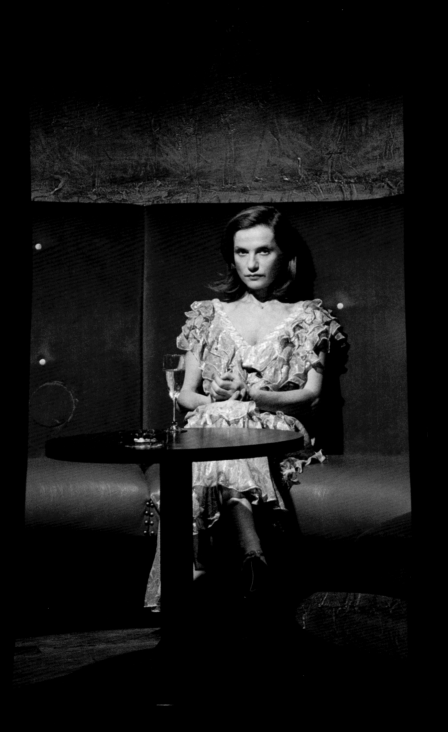

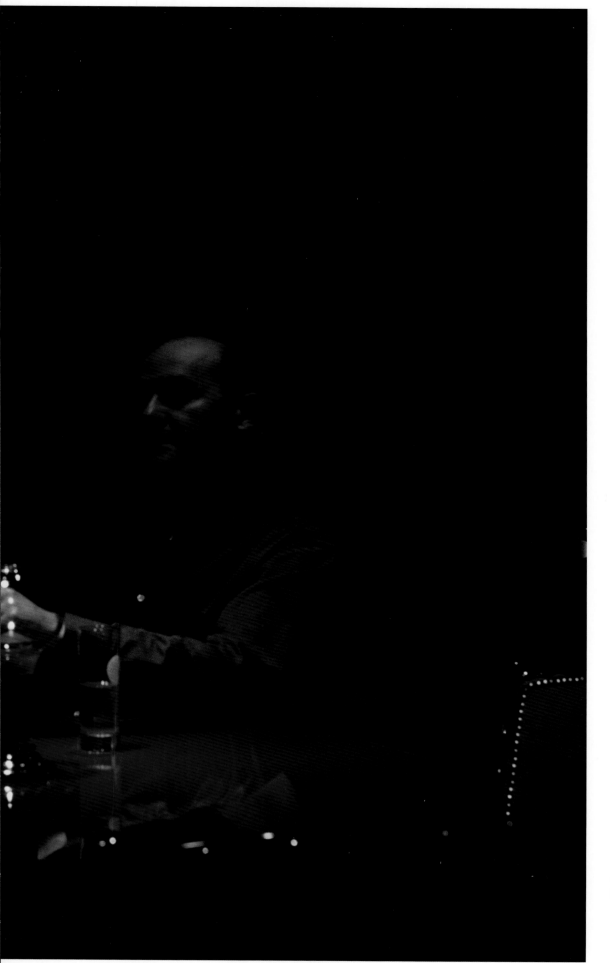

PHILIP-LORCA
DICORCIA. *2004*

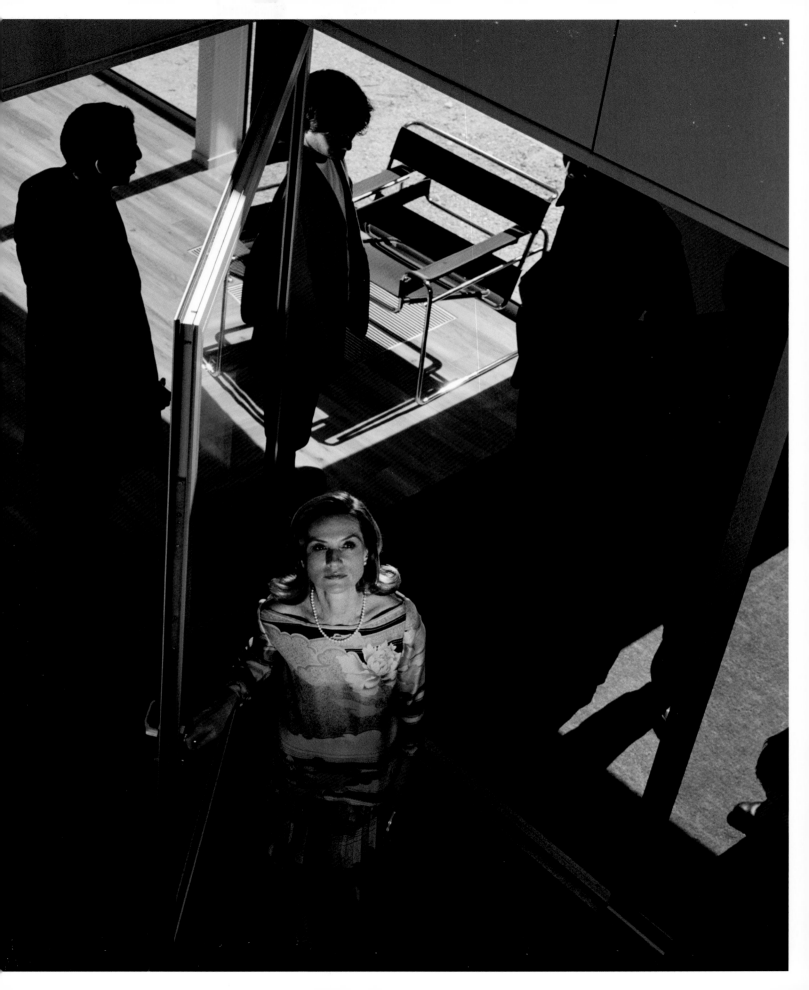

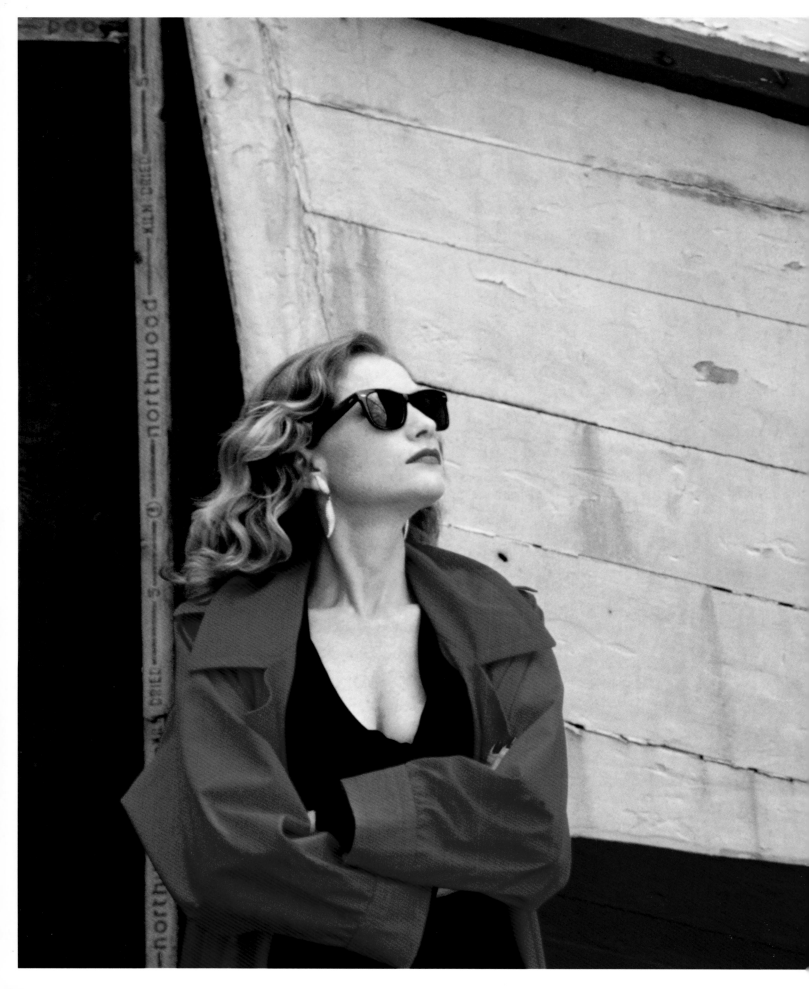

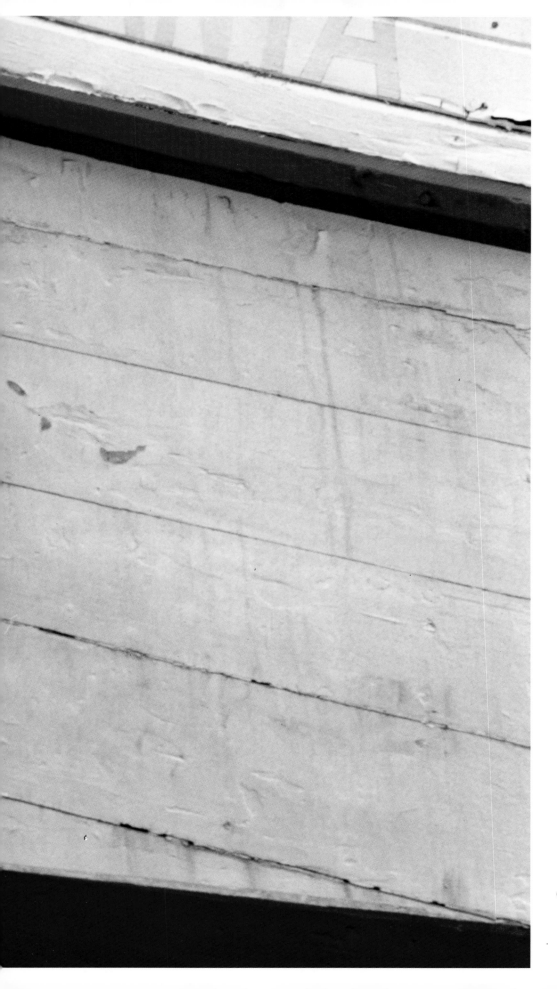

GEORGE WHITEAR. *1986*

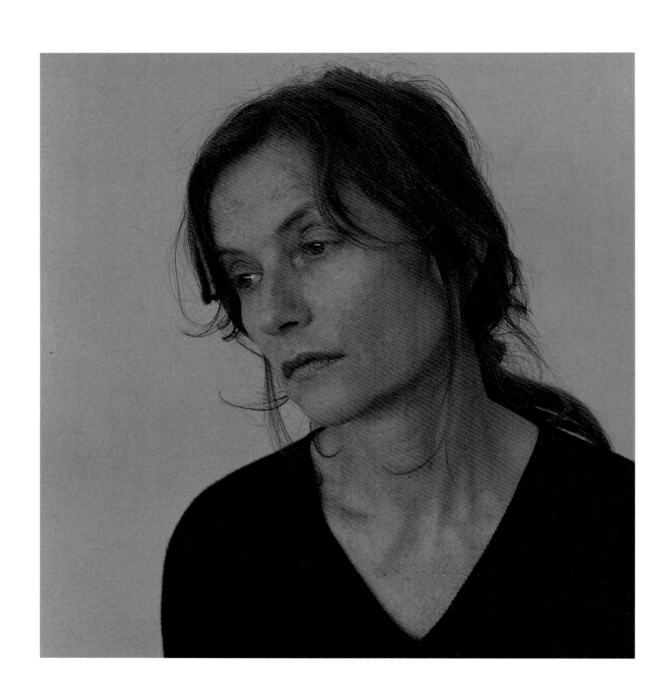

PATRICK FAIGENBAUM. *2005*

144

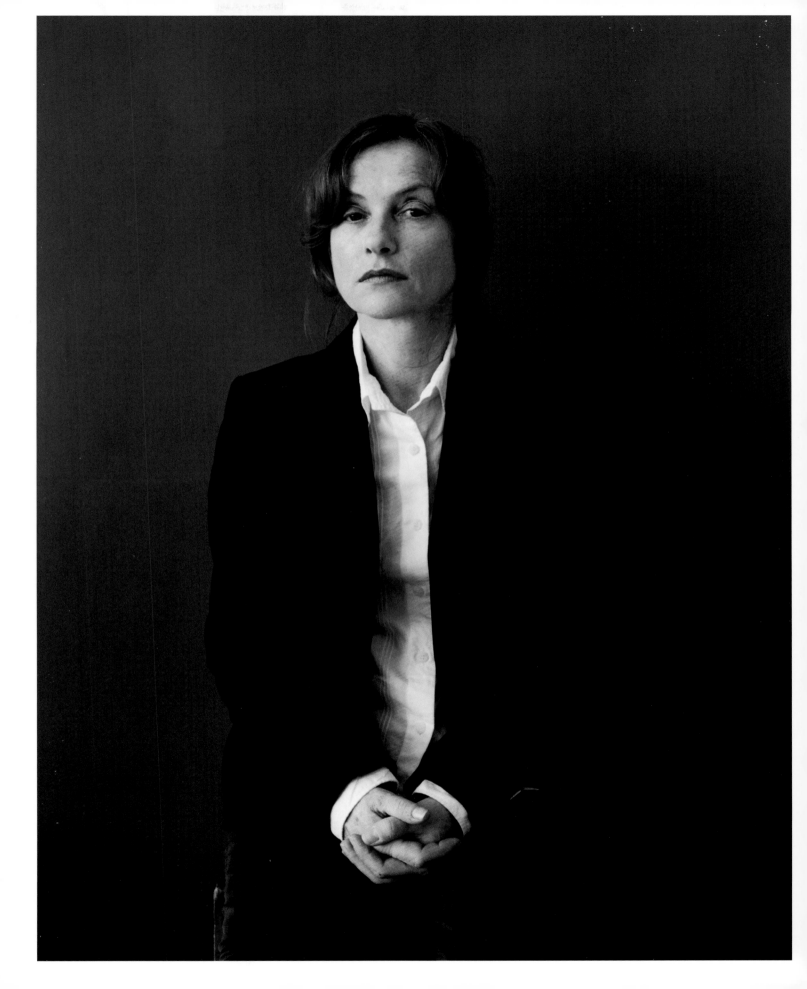

JOEL-PETER WITKIN, *2004*

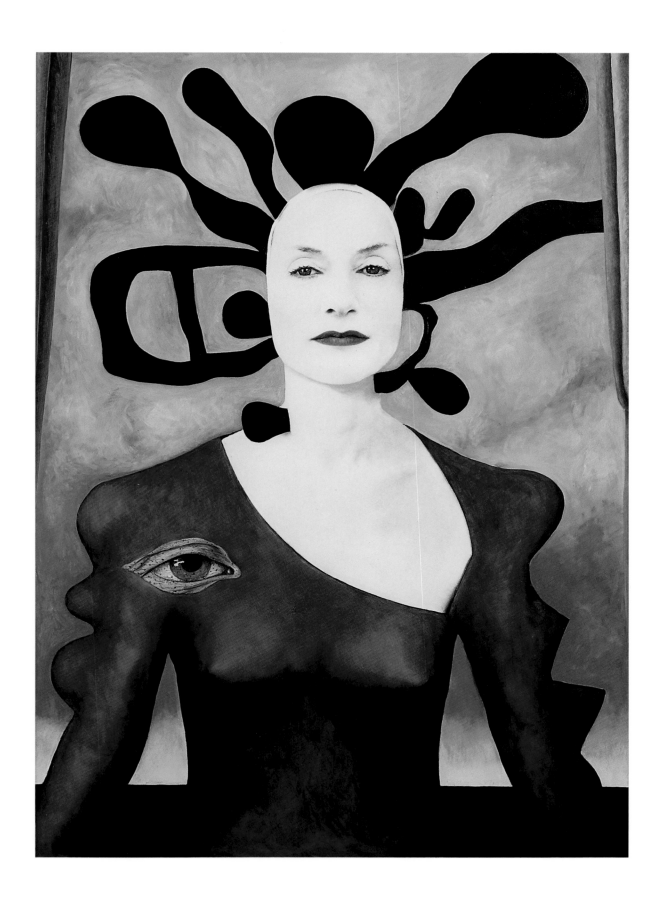

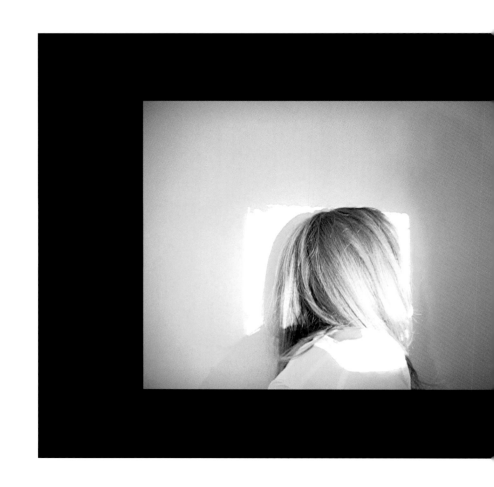

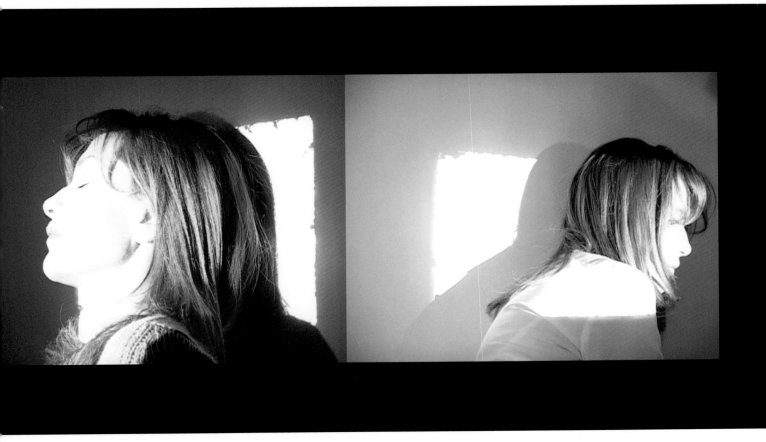

ANGE LECCIA. *2004*

149

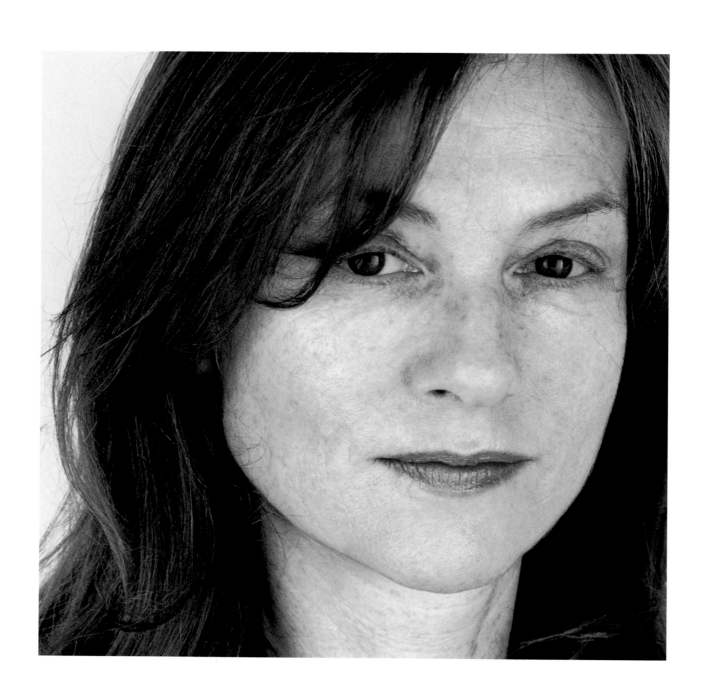

RONI HORN, *2005*

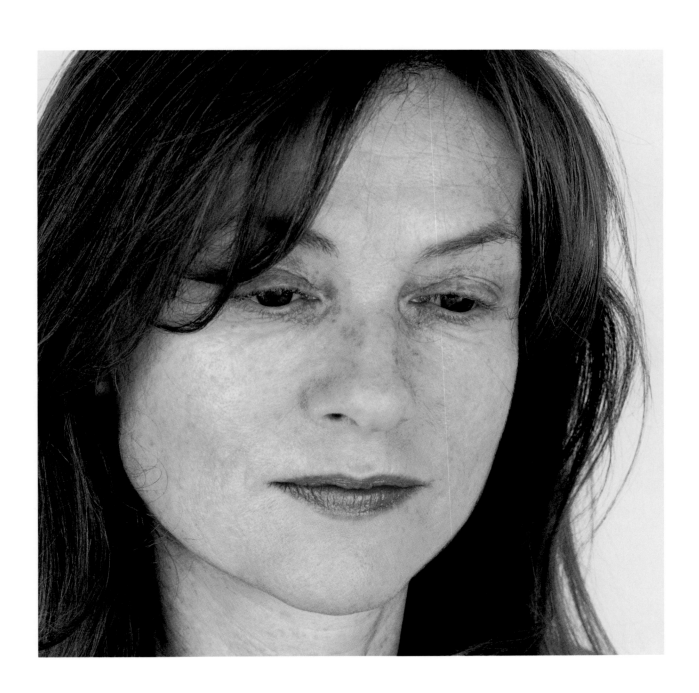

RONI HORN, *2005*

151

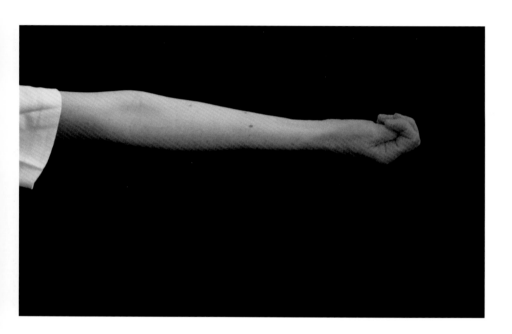

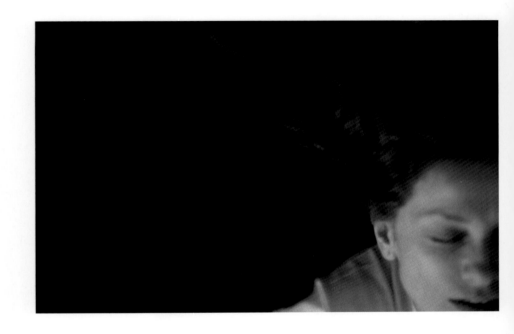

HEDI SLIMANE, *2005*

153

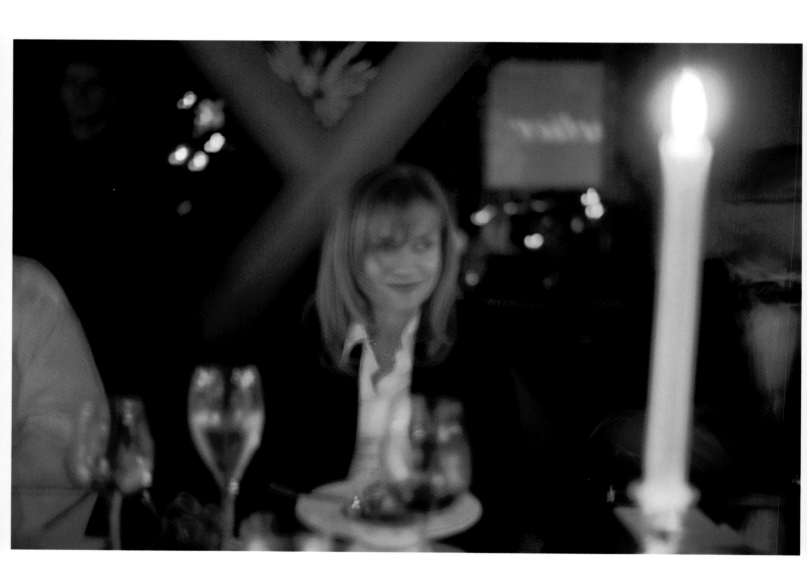

NAN GOLDIN. *2004*

154

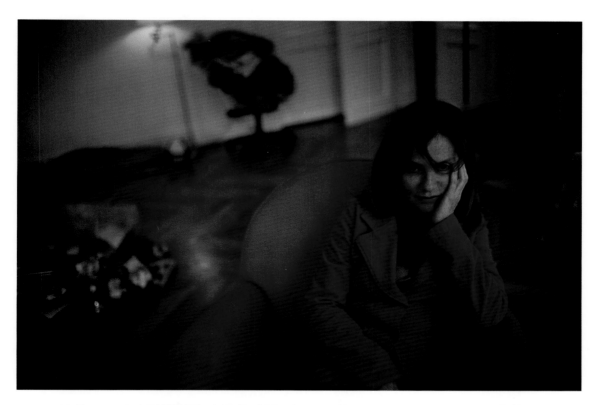

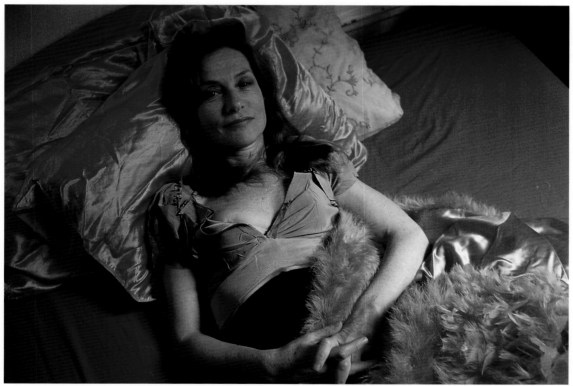

NAN GOLDIN. 2004. 2005

NAN GOLDIN, *2004*

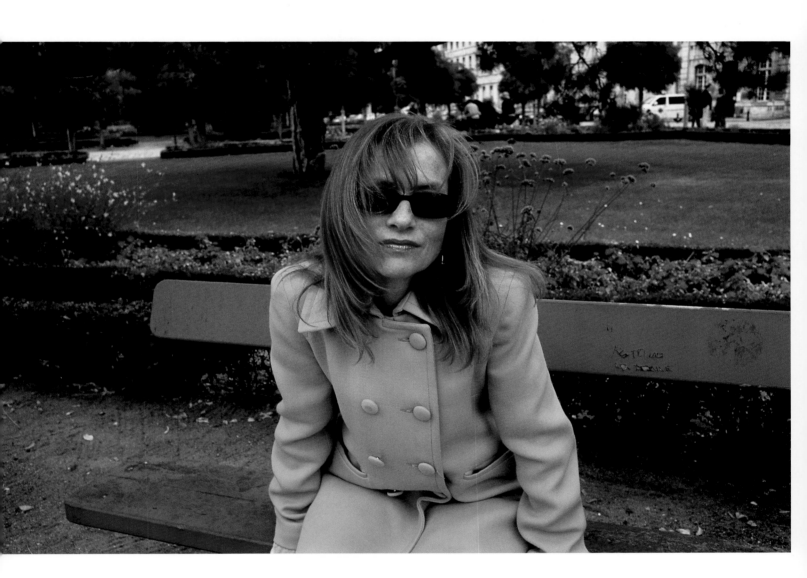

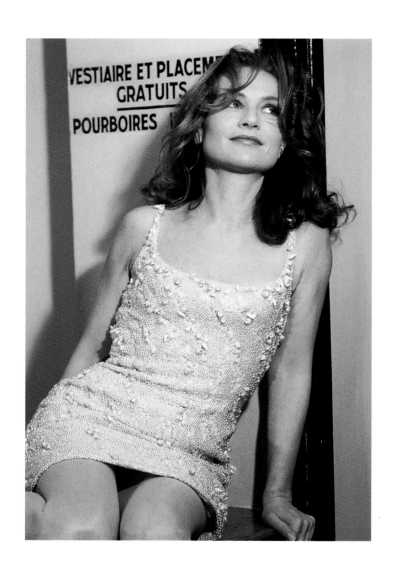

BETTINA RHEIMS, *1992*
ANTOINE D'AGATA, *2003*

158

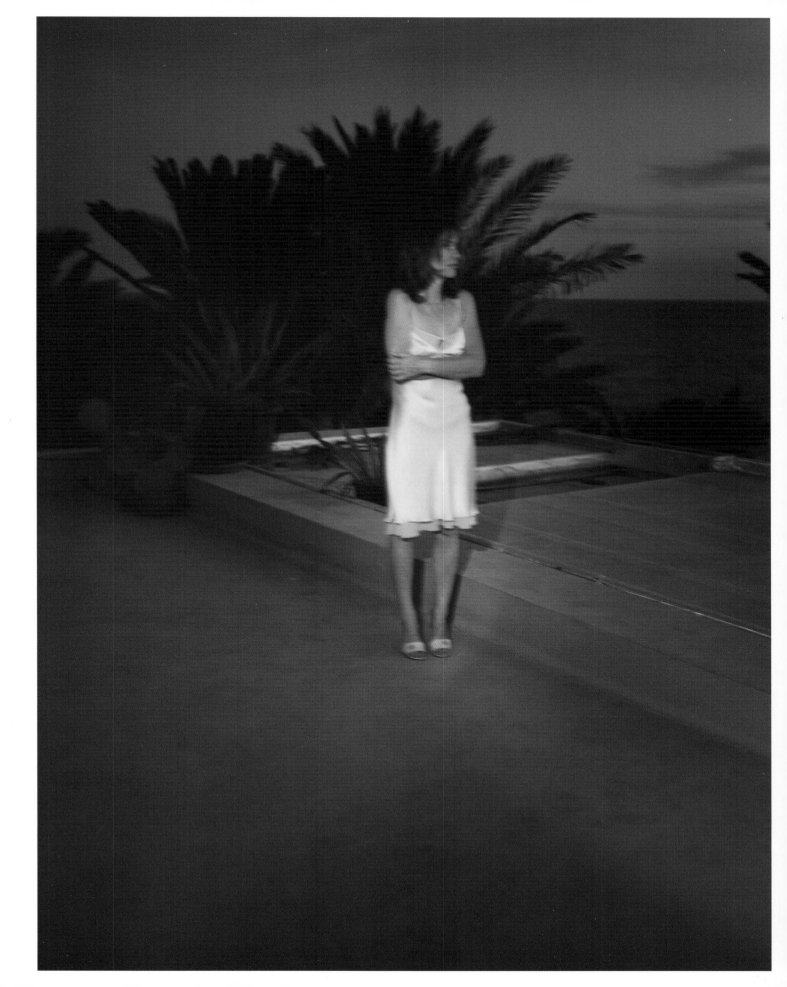

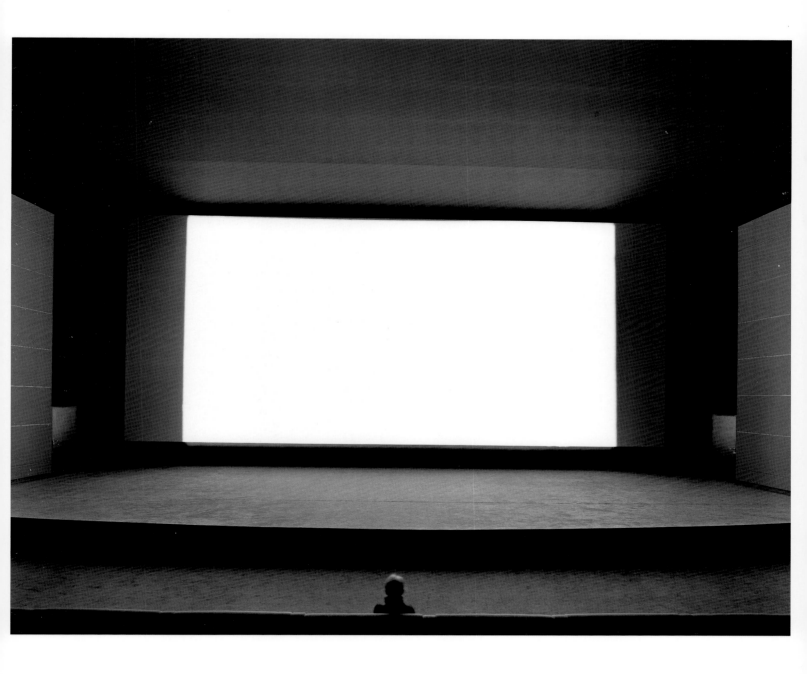

PHOTOGRAPHER BIOGRAPHIES

Antoine d'Agata
Born 1961 in Marseille; lives in Paris
Antoine d'Agata spent ten years living outside France, residing in London, Mexico, and finally New York, where he attended the School of the International Center of Photography (ICP). He joined the Magnum agency in 2004. "I am not interested in the way a photographer looks at the world, but rather in his most intimate relations with it." he said.

Richard Avedon
New York, 1923–San Antonio, Texas, 2004
Richard Avedon first worked as a photographer while in the merchant marine during the Second World War. His first fashion photographs were published in 1944 in *Harper's Bazaar,* and he devised a new style by portraying models in street settings. He joined *Vogue* in 1965. A great portrait photographer, Avedon here has revealed the "emotional landscape" of his model's face and body.

Arnaud Baumann
Born 1953 in Réunion; lives in Paris
Arnaud Baumann studied architecture at the École Nationale Supérieure des Beaux-Arts (School of Fine Arts) in Paris. He is well known for his "videocaptures," which he first made for the newspaper *Libération* at the forty-fifth Cannes Film Festival, in 1992. He broke free of the still photographic image by videotaping his subjects and then extracting stills from his videos.

Carole Bellaïche
Born 1964 in Paris, where she lives
A portrait photographer first and foremost, Carole Bellaïche worked for the *Cahiers du Cinéma* for ten years and now works for various magazines. She also is working on a project on the subject of the nude and the city.

Édouard Boubat
Paris, 1923–Paris, 1999
A photoengraver like Robert Doisneau, Édouard Boubat exhibited his first photographs with Doisneau in 1949. In 1951 an exhibition at La Hune gallery with Brassaï, Isis, Facchetti, and Doisneau earned him his first reportage assignment, portraying the craftsmen of Paris for the magazine *Réalités.* Thus began a series of journeys spanning five continents. Fascinated by people and by life, he immortalized "the moments when nothing is happening except everyday life."

Jean-Christian Bourcart
Born 1960 in Colmar, France; lives in New York
A photojournalist since 1985, Jean-Christian Bourcart joined the Rapho agency in 1990 and has worked for many French and international newspapers. He is also a portrait photographer and has photographed the most inaccessible subjects, such as prostitutes in Frankfurt brothels.

Guy Bourdin
Paris, 1928–Paris, 1991
Guy Bourdin learned photography while serving in the military in Senegal in 1948. He received his first commission in 1955 from French *Vogue,* with which he worked for the next thirty years. In 1967 he was asked to handle the advertising campaign for Charles Jourdan shoes, which made him famous. His images, which are provocative and disturbing, radically changed the course of fashion photography.

Jérôme Brézillon
Born 1964 in Paris, where he lives
Jérôme Brézillon has devoted himself to photojournalism since 1981. A member of the Métis agency, he has covered war in Bosnia, Cyprus, and Northern Ireland. He has also produced reportages on oil slicks, everyday life at the Institut Médico-Légal in Paris, and the death penalty in the United States.

Henri Cartier-Bresson
Chanteloup, France, 1908–Montjustin, France, 2004
Henri Cartier-Bresson took up painting in 1923 and photography in 1931. A photojournalist, he cofounded the Magnum agency in 1947. Throughout his career he traveled the world with his Leica, capturing images in Africa, Eastern Europe, the USSR, and Mexico. In 2003 he set up the Henri Cartier-Bresson Foundation in Paris. He was a champion of the "decisive moment." "Portraying the world requires ... concentration, sensitivity, and a sense of geometry," he said.

Ronald Chammah
Born 1951 in Beirut; lives in Paris
Italian by adoption, Ronald Chammah since 1982 has worked in Paris as a film producer and director. He is a photography enthusiast and an amateur photographer in his own right.

Jean-Philippe Charbonnier
Paris, 1921–Paris, 2004
Jean-Philippe Charbonnier discovered photography in 1939 in the studio of the famous cinema portraitist Sam Lévin. As a photojournalist for the monthly *Réalités* between 1950 and 1974 he traveled the world, from Africa to Asia. From 1975 on he devoted himself to the inhabitants of the Marais district of Paris, where he lived, convinced that the exotic was to be found "on the corner of the street."

Pénélope Chauvelot
Born 1950 in Neuilly, France; lives in Rome
Pénélope Chauvelot was introduced to photography through Marie-Laure de Decker and Raymond Depardon. Beginning in 1978 she produced reportages for the Sygma agency from Vietnam, Cambodia, and Lebanon. Since 1985 she has worked for interior design and architecture magazines, as well as in the theater and in films.

Michel Comte
Born 1954 in Zurich; lives in Paris
From a very early age Michel Comte was interested in the photographs of Man Ray and Weegee. He worked at photographic restoration before settling in Paris, where he was soon entrusted with the Ungaro advertising campaign. From 1979 on his work appeared in international magazines. Comte is also a photojournalist and has traveled with Red Cross missions to Pakistan, Bosnia, and Afghanistan.

Roger Corbeau
Haguenau, France, 1908–Paris, 1995
Roger Corbeau began his career in 1933 as Marcel Pagnol's on-set stills photographer, a position he held for ten years. He then worked on more than 160 films with the most distinguished directors, from Abel Gance to Claude Chabrol, and from Jean Cocteau to Orson Welles. Fascinated by actors, he worked by staging them, then photographing their faces.

Bruce Davidson
Born 1933 in Oak Park, Illinois; lives in New York
Bruce Davidson met Henri Cartier-Bresson while doing military service in Paris. He worked for *Life* magazine in 1957, joined the Magnum agency in 1958, and worked for *Vogue* for some years. In 1964 he began a photographic series on people living on the margins of society in New York. He frequented shelters and captured the faces of people living in subway tunnels.

Marie-Laure de Decker
Born 1947 in Algeria; lives in Rabastens, France
Marie-Laure de Decker began her career by taking portraits of Man Ray and Orson Welles. During the 1970s she headed to Saigon, to cover the Vietnam War. Thereafter she joined the Gamma agency and traveled the world. Always a multidisciplinary photographer (shooting films, fashion, wars, and her own surroundings), for the last three years de Decker has been making a study of the Walencouy tribe of southern Chad.

Patrick Demarchelier
Born 1944 in Paris; lives in New York
Patrick Demarchelier began his photography career in Paris. He left France in 1975 to settle in New York. In 1992 he became chief photographer of *Harper's Bazaar*. In 2004 he began an exclusive relationship with *Vogue* and *Vanity Fair*.

Raymond Depardon
Born 1942 in Villefranche-sur-Saône, France; lives in Paris
As a child Raymond Depardon photographed his parents' farm. He became a paparazzo, then a photojournalist, and in 1966 founded the Gamma agency with Gilles Caron. He embarked on a career as a documentary filmmaker and joined the Magnum agency in 1978. A witness to his times, he portrays the world in uncompromising terms and links news photography directly to the text.

Philip-Lorca DiCorcia
Born 1953 in Hartford, Connecticut; lives in New York
Philip-Lorca DiCorcia studied under Nan Goldin at the School of the Museum of Fine Arts, Boston, from 1975, and later at Yale University. His work initially centered on photographing those close to him but progressively shifted toward society and the individual: His lens focuses on faces or people. DiCorcia's work combines documentary realism with the fictions of cinema and advertising.

Robert Doisneau
Gentilly, France, 1912–Paris, 1994
An engraver and lithographer, Robert Doisneau learned industrial photography at Renault, then joined the Rapho agency in 1946. Always in search of the ephemeral, the photographer who shot the famous *Baiser de l'Hôtel de Ville (Kiss Outside Paris Town Hall)* immortalized the humor and charm of the inhabitants of a sentimental, working-class Paris. His images, imbued with humanity, often convey his hatred of war.

Claudine Doury
Born 1959 in Blois, France; lives in Paris
After working for ten years as a photo researcher at the newspaper *Libération*, Claudine Doury produced her first big reportage in Siberia, immediately after the fall of the Berlin Wall. She joined the Vu agency in 1991. Doury captures the fragility of being and has an interest in Siberian peoples and traditions that are vanishing.

Richard Dumas
Lives in Rennes, France
After completing a doctorate in robotics and playing in the group Sax Pustuls, Richard Dumas began his photography career shooting pictures at rock concerts. He joined the Vu agency in 1994. A great portraitist, he plays with contrast and produces iconic images ringed with light.

William Eggleston
Born 1939 in Memphis, where he lives
After experimenting with black-and-white, William Eggleston dedicated himself in 1969 to color photography, of which he is regarded as one of the American masters. His images, balanced somewhere between a look at everyday American life and art photography, depict everything from cars to landscapes, streets to supermarkets. Eggleston has also taken photographs in Kenya, China, and England. His composition is unique and precise, and he chooses disorienting viewpoints.

Elliott Erwitt
Born 1928 in Paris; lives in New York
The son of Russian immigrants, in 1939 Elliott Erwitt left France for the United States, where he studied photography and film. He met Robert Capa during military service in France, and in 1954 joined the Magnum agency. Today he is known for his photographs of dogs, which emphasize "the animal nature of humans and the humanity of animals."

Patrick Faigenbaum
Born 1954 in Paris, where he lives
Patrick Faigenbaum took up photography after studying painting. Between 1985 and 1987 he was resident at the Académie de France in Rome. He is interested in genealogy and photographs Italian aristocracy. Lately his work has focused more on his own history; he shoots portraits of friends and family.

Martine Franck
Born 1938 in Antwerp, Belgium; lives in Paris
Martine Franck took her first photographs during a journey to China, Japan, and India. She began to work freelance for *Vogue*, *Life*, and the *New York Times*; she cofounded the Viva agency in 1972. In 1983 she became an associate member of the Magnum agency. Franck favors precise composition and emotional restraint, to "encourage reflection."

Robert Frank
Born 1924 in Zurich; lives in Nova Scotia, Canada
Robert Frank settled in New York in 1947. He worked as a fashion photographer and reporter for *Life* and *Harper's Bazaar*. Associated with the Beat Generation, he traveled around the United States for two years. With his photographs, seemingly badly composed and poorly lit, Frank revolutionized the foundations of photojournalism, both technically and in terms of content.

Leonard Freed
Born 1929 in Brooklyn, New York; lives in New York
Leonard Freed first wanted to be a painter. In 1954 he attended seminars on photography held by Alexei Brodovitch, artistic director of *Harper's Bazaar*, which changed his course. Freed achieved fame documenting the American civil rights movement. A member of the Magnum agency, he teaches photography at The New School in New York.

Claude Gassian
Born 1949 in Paris, where he lives
Since 1970 Claude Gassian has been photographing musicians, including Lou Reed, Bob Dylan, Prince, and Bob Marley. Far from being flamboyant portraits, his photographs are often oblique, in black-and-white, and reflect the atmosphere of life on tour.

Ralph Gibson
Born 1939 in Los Angeles; lives in New York
Ralph Gibson worked as assistant to Dorothea Lange and later to Robert Frank. He joined the Magnum agency, worked in fashion and advertising, and in 1970 devoted himself to art photography. He works primarily in black-and-white and draws inspiration from everyday life; using elements of reality as his starting point, he creates surreal effects. His work, which explores the human body from every angle, is marked by great sensuality.

Nan Goldin
Born 1953 in Washington, D.C.; lives in New York, Berlin, and Paris
Deeply affected by a family tragedy, Nan Goldin produced her first reportage, on the subject of her family, at age eighteen. In 1978 she embarked on *The Ballad of Sexual Dependency*, recording episodes of her own life in underground circles in the United States and Europe.

Lucien Hervé
Born 1910 in Hódmezővàsàrhely, Hungary; lives in Paris
A Hungarian Jew who emigrated to France in 1929, Lucien Hervé was a tailor, pianist, film director, and painter before he became a photographer. From 1949 to 1965 he was Le Corbusier's personal photographer. His works are unique in their extremely stark contrast and almost total absence of human figures.

Noelle Hoeppe
Born 1958 in Paris, where she lives
Noelle Hoeppe studied applied arts in Paris, followed by photography and film in New York, where she lived for ten years. Her black-and-white photographs depict a universe imbued with sensuality and eroticism. She returned to Paris in 1990 and added color to her palette, starting with a series of very large still lifes. Hoeppe works for a number of magazines and advertising agencies.

Robin Holland
Born in Yonkers, New York; lives in New York
Robin Holland photographed the director Wim Wenders in 1982 and was subsequently employed as stills photographer on his film *Paris, Texas*. She also worked on the films of Claire Denis and Agnès Godard. Holland describes herself as a portraitist obsessed by cinema.

Roni Horn
Born 1955 in New York, where she lives
Roni Horn divides her life between two contrasting worlds: New York and Iceland. The latter has inspired several series of photographs as well as drawings, objects, sculptures, and videos. Her work reveals her twinned concerns: change and the failure to achieve a stable identity.

Frank Horvat
Born 1928 in Abbazia, Italy; lives in Paris
After working as a news photographer for *Paris Match* and *Life*, Frank Horvat specialized in fashion photography, posing his models in the street. In 1989 he began to work on a more personal series of photographs.

Dominique Issermann
Born 1947 in Paris, where she lives
Dominique Issermann began in reportage, but soon became "photographer to the stars." She has produced advertising campaigns (both photographs and film) for Sonia Rykiel, Dior, and Cartier, as well as music videos.

Douglas Kirkland
Born 1934 in Toronto; lives in Hollywood, California
Douglas Kirkland worked for *Look* and *Life* magazines and photographed such celebrities as Marilyn Monroe and Marlene Dietrich. He innovated by posing his models outdoors and shooting them in a photojournalistic style. The stills photographer on several feature films, including *Titanic* and *Moulin Rouge!*, he has traveled the world, producing reportages on such subjects as astronomy in Chile and fashion in Bali.

Thomas Klausmann
Born 1957 in Ludwigshafen, Germany; lives in Ireland
Thomas Klausmann began his career as a fashion and advertising photographer, and then became a film stills photographer. After a long period in Paris, where he worked closely with the film director Claude Chabrol, he left the profession in 1991. He settled in San Francisco, where he opened a restaurant, before moving to Ireland.

Nick Knight
Born 1958 in Great Britain; lives in London
Under contract with the American edition of *Vogue*, Nick Knight also has worked for a number of international magazines, including *Vanity Fair* and *The Face*, and shot advertising campaigns for Alexander McQueen and Yves Saint Laurent. In 2000 he founded SHOWstudio.com and produced album covers for David Bowie and Massive Attack.

Josef Koudelka
Born 1938 in Boskovice, Czechoslovakia; lives in France
Josef Koudelka was an engineer before becoming a photographer. He produced a reportage on the Soviet invasion of Prague in August 1968. In 1971 he went to Paris and joined the Magnum agency. His favorite subject is Gypsies. In 1986, when he accepted a commission from the French Ministry of the Interior for a project on the country's urban and rural landscapes, he began using a panoramic camera. His black-and-white prints are filled with tragedy and optimism.

Brigitte Lacombe
Lives in New York
Brigitte Lacombe was chief photographer for the Goodman Theater in Chicago in 1983 and for New York's Lincoln Center Theater in 1985–92. Fascinated by portraiture and by travel, she spent sixteen years traversing the globe for *Condé Nast Traveler* magazine. Lacombe is also a film stills photographer. She has worked for Federico Fellini, Steven Spielberg, and Martin Scorsese.

Jacques Henri Lartigue
Courbevoie, France, 1884–Nice, France, 1986
Initially recognized as a painter, Jacques Henri Lartigue published his first photographs in 1954. He captured moments of happiness, working first in black-and-white and then in color, as well as with stereoscopic images, panoramic cameras, and the autochrome process, and chronicled his life in albums of photographs.

William Laxton
Born 1961 in Orléans, France; lives in Taipei, Taiwan
William Laxton began as a photographer for *Première*, then worked for publications such as *Studio* and *Le Monde*. He is fascinated by films and by Asia. He is training to become a Buddhist monk but returns to Europe each year for the Cannes Film Festival, which he has covered for the last ten years.

Ange Leccia
Born 1952 in Minerviù, Corsica; lives in Paris
Ange Leccia first made an impact in the 1980s with his "arrangements" of objects such as bricks, cars, television sets, and motorcycles. Inspired by the Mediterranean, he is a videographer, a painter, and an installation artist. Leccia runs the Pavillon, a teaching institute at the Palais de Tokyo, a contemporary arts center in Paris.

Annie Leibovitz
Born 1949 in Waterbury, Connecticut; lives in New York
Annie Leibovitz achieved widespread fame with her 1980 portrait of John Lennon and Yoko Ono for the cover of *Rolling Stone*, for which she had been chief photographer since 1973. She joined *Vanity Fair* in 1983. She stages each of the stars she photographs, giving them each a specific role in a particular setting.

Peter Lindbergh
Born 1944 in Duisburg, Germany; lives in Paris
Peter Lindbergh studied painting in Berlin and became interested in conceptual art. In 1978 the German magazine *Stern* published his first fashion photographs. He works on advertising campaigns as well as documentaries. Specializing in black-and-white, Lindbergh produces highly original photographs inspired by cinema.

Anne-Marie Miéville
Born 1945 in Lausanne, Switzerland; lives in Rolle, Switzerland
Anne-Marie Miéville has written and directed about fifteen feature-length films, including *Mon Cher Sujet* (1988) and *Après la Réconciliation* (2000). Since 1972 she has worked on a number of films with Jean-Luc Godard, in roles including poster photographer, actress, producer, codirector, and screenwriter.

Sarah Moon
Born 1941 in Paris, where she lives
Sarah Moon began in fashion as a model and took photographs of her friends. Her first photography assignment, for Cacharel in 1967, was followed by commissions from various fashion magazines. Her work reflects a dreamy, poetic personal world; in her images "the maleficent is juxtaposed with beauty."

Pete Moss
Born 1960 in London, where he lives
An artist and photographer, Pete Moss studied photography at Bournemouth College of Art and Goldsmith College, an art school in London. He has worked for numerous publications around the world.

Helmut Newton
Berlin, 1920–Hollywood, California, 2004
Helmut Newton left school at an early age to devote himself to photography. He worked for the most prestigious fashion magazines and made portraits of such celebrities as Ava Gardner, Salvador Dali, and Andy Warhol. His provocative, unconventional work offers a personal view of the worlds of fashion, money, and power.

Gueorgui Pinkhassov
Born 1952 in Moscow; lives in Paris
Cameraman and later stills photographer for Mosfilm, Gueorgui Pinkhassov left Moscow in 1985 for Paris, where he entered the Magnum agency. He has covered events all over the world—notably the collapse of the Soviet Union—for various magazines. He frequently uses shadows to break light and shoots his images out of focus.

Sylvia Plachy
Born 1943 in Budapest; lives in New York
Sylvia Plachy fled Hungary with her parents in 1956, settling in the United States. For the last forty years she has photographed New York, chiefly in black-and-white, and contributed to numerous magazines. She regularly travels in her native country and elsewhere in Eastern Europe. Her book *Self-Portrait with Cows Going Home* is her photographic and written account of this personal quest.

Bernard Plossu
Born 1945 in Dalat, Vietnam; lives in La Ciotat, France
Bernard Plossu took his first photographs at age thirteen, using a Brownie Flash, in the Sahara. In 1965 he joined an ethnological mission to Mexico, where he traveled constantly and over long distances. The coherence and fluidity of Plossu's vision constitute an invitation to travel and discover other people.

Len Prince
Born 1953 in Detroit, Michigan; lives in New York
Len Prince has directed advertising campaigns for Estée Lauder and Cartier, among others. In 1994 he photographed film stars in Los Angeles's legendary Château Marmont hotel, imitating the classic black-and-white Hollywood portraits of the 1920s, 1930s, and 1940s.

Guy Le Querrec
Born 1941 in Paris, where he lives
A passionate jazz lover, Guy Le Querrec's first photographs were of musicians in London in the late 1950s. He traveled Francophone Africa for the periodical *Jeune Afrique*. He cofounded the Viva agency and was a member until 1976, when he rejoined the Magnum agency. "Jazz is a way of life, a way of walking the tightrope of chance in quest of the imaginary, which contains improvisation and inquisitiveness," he said.

Bettina Rheims
Born 1952 in Paris, where she lives
The daughter of the writer Maurice Rheims, Bettina Rheims was a model who turned to photography at the end of the 1970s. She makes portraits of women, nightlife, and celebrities such as Charlotte Rampling; she is also official photographer of Jacques Chirac, the president of France. She has published many books, including *I.N.R.I.*, a series of photographs depicting the life of Jesus, whose release provoked controversy.

Marc Riboud
Born 1923 in Lyon, France; lives in Paris
An engineer who trained at the École Centrale in Lyon, Marc Riboud decided to devote himself to photography in 1951. In 1953 he met Henri Cartier-Bresson and Robert Capa, who invited him to join the Magnum agency. He then traveled all over Asia, the USSR, Algeria, and sub-Saharan Africa. He has worked independently since 1980.

Herb Ritts
Los Angeles, 1952–Los Angeles, 2002
During the 1970s Herb Ritts photographed friends who worked in the movies. In the 1980s and 1990s he shot the biggest stars, including Richard Gere, Jack Nicholson, and Madonna. He also worked on advertising campaigns for large fashion houses. Herb Ritts's photographs reflect the life and light of southern California.

Karin Rocholl
Born and lives in Berlin
After working as a fashion editor for a number of magazines, Karin Rocholl decided to become a photographer in 1982. Since 1988 she has worked for *Stern*, where she devotes herself to portraits of actors, writers, and painters.

Willy Ronis
Born 1910 in Paris, where he lives
Family obligations drew Willy Ronis to join his father's photographic studio in 1932, but he decided to become an independent photojournalist in 1937. He produced many socially conscious reportages, notably on the children of the Belleville and Ménilmontant districts of Paris. Commissioned by numerous magazines, such as *Le Monde Illustré*, *Life*, and *L'Illustration*, he covered business and fashion. Ronis is a member of the Rapho agency.

Paolo Roversi
Born 1947 in Ravenna, Italy; lives in Paris
A former reporter, Paolo Roversi settled in Paris in 1973. Since then his elegant style, with gentle lighting and sophisticated colors, has appeared in many international magazines. He emphasizes emotion to create a world that hovers between dream and reality.

Lise Sarfati
Born 1958 in Algeria; lives in Paris
In 1989 Lise Sarfati visited Russia, where she was fascinated by places that bore the marks of history, such as converted factories and psychiatric hospitals, and by young people. Since then she has produced a series on American adolescents.

Ferdinando Scianna
Born 1946 in Bagheria, Sicily; lives in Milan
Sicily was the subject of Ferdinando Scianna's first attempts at photography. He began working as a photojournalist in Milan in 1966, a career he continued in Paris. He joined the Magnum agency in 1989. Scianna works in fashion as well as reportage. He often plays with reflections and shadows to produce unreal images.

Jeanloup Sieff
Paris, 1933–Paris, 2000
Jeanloup Sieff began taking photographs in 1954, inspired by France's New Wave cinema. He worked for *Elle* magazine and the Magnum agency, then lived in New York from 1961 to 1966. After returning to Paris he worked for a number of fashion magazines. He often chooses muted light and intimate spaces for his portraits.

Hedi Slimane
Born 1968 in Paris, where he lives
Hedi Slimane studied art history at the École du Louvre. In 1997 he joined Yves Saint Laurent as director of collections, and then became the company's artistic director. Since 2000 he has been creative director of Christian Dior's men's collections. He is fascinated by rock music and photographs its stars.

Hiroshi Sugimoto
Born 1948 in Tokyo; lives in New York
Based in New York since 1974, Hiroshi Sugimoto has traveled all over the world to make his "series" on architecture, wax figures, and industrial machinery. Using an American-made wooden device, which resembles a nineteenth-century camera body, and very long exposure times, he accentuates details and lighting and plays on the perception of time.

Juergen Teller
Born 1964 in Erlangen, Germany; lives in London
Juergen Teller began his career photographing people in the music world. His first fashion photographs were for magazines and fashion houses' ad campaigns. He bases his work on the dialogue he establishes with his models.

Michel Vanden Eeckhoudt
Born 1947 in Brussels, where he lives
A member of the Vu agency since its creation in 1985, Michel Vanden Eeckhoudt is a photojournalist who regularly contributes to the newspaper *Libération*. His work is both poetic and dramatic.

Pascal Victor
Born 1955 in Falaise, France; lives in Paris
Specializing in entertainment photography, Pascal Victor has produced portraits for French magazines and newspapers such as *Le Monde*, *Télérama*, and *Libération*. He has collaborated with many artists, including Peter Brook, Claude Regy, Jean-Marie Patte, and Alain Françon. He is a member of the MAXPPP agency.

George Whitear
George Whitear, a film stills photographer, has worked on the sets of *Star Wars, Episode V–The Empire Strikes Back* (1980), *Dune* (1984), and the James Bond film *Tomorrow Never Dies* (1997). He photographed Isabelle Huppert in 1987 on the set of Curtis Hanson's *The Bedroom Window*.

Joel-Peter Witkin
Born 1939 in New York, where he lives
Joel-Peter Witkin made his first attempts at photography at the age of sixteen and studied photography at the University of New Mexico in 1975. He has taken (and retouched) many photographs inspired by the paintings of Goya, Rubens, and Bosch, often creating nightmarish visions.

Hugues de Wurstemberger
Born 1955 in Bern, Switzerland; lives in Brussels
A former Swiss Guard, Hugues de Wurstemberger joined the Vu agency in 1986. He covered film and theater festivals for *Libération*; he also traveled and photographed in El Salvador, the Philippines, Algeria, Ethiopia, and Zambia. In recent years he has photographed his children, Pauline and Juju.

BIOGRAPHICAL NOTES BY ELSA JANSSEN

ACKNOWLEDGMENTS

Thanks to
Dominique Bourgois, Hervé Mikaeloff, Paolo Roversi,
Nicolas Ghesquière, Marin Karmitz, Almine Rech,
Jacqueline Chambord, Nora Coblence, Karine Louesdon,
Jacques Binsztok.

CAPTIONS

Page 20: Elfriede Jelinek
Page 125: Jean-Louis Murat
Page 126: Werner Schroeter
Page 128 (bottom): Bob Wilson and Pierre Soulages